Mastering the Microsoft Kinect

Body Tracking, Object Detection, and the Azure Cloud Services

Vangos Pterneas

Apress®

Mastering the Microsoft Kinect: Body Tracking, Object Detection, and the Azure Cloud Services

Vangos Pterneas
New York City, NY, USA

ISBN-13 (pbk): 978-1-4842-8069-0
https://doi.org/10.1007/978-1-4842-8070-6

ISBN-13 (electronic): 978-1-4842-8070-6

Managing Director, Apress Media LLC: Welmoed Spahr
Acquisitions Editor: Jonathan Gennick
Development Editor: Laura Berendson
Coordinating Editor: Jill Balzano

Cover image designed by Freepik (www.freepik.com)

Distributed to the book trade worldwide by Springer Science+Business Media LLC, 1 New York Plaza, Suite 4600, New York, NY 10004. Phone 1-800-SPRINGER, fax (201) 348-4505, e-mail orders-ny@springer-sbm. com, or visit www.springeronline.com. Apress Media, LLC is a California LLC and the sole member (owner) is Springer Science + Business Media Finance Inc (SSBM Finance Inc). SSBM Finance Inc is a **Delaware** corporation.

For information on translations, please e-mail booktranslations@springernature.com; for reprint, paperback, or audio rights, please e-mail bookpermissions@springernature.com.

Apress titles may be purchased in bulk for academic, corporate, or promotional use. eBook versions and licenses are also available for most titles. For more information, reference our Print and eBook Bulk Sales web page at http://www.apress.com/bulk-sales.

Any source code or other supplementary material referenced by the author in this book is available to readers on GitHub.

Printed on acid-free paper

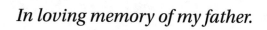
In loving memory of my father.

Table of Contents

About the Author

Vangos Pterneas is a professional software engineer and an award-winning Microsoft Most Valuable Professional. Since 2012, Vangos has been helping Fortune 500 companies and ambitious startups create demanding motion-tracking applications. He is obsessive about analyzing and modeling every aspect of the human motion using computer vision and mathematics. Kinect programming started as a hobby and quickly evolved into a full-time business. Vangos shares his passion by regularly publishing articles and open source projects that help fellow developers understand the fascinating Kinect technology.

About the Technical Reviewer

Quentin Miller is Principal Program Manager in Azure AI Platform, Microsoft. Quentin was the Program Manager for software development on Project Kinect for Azure that led to the development and release of Azure Kinect in July 2019. He now leads the Azure Kinect product program. Quentin is also responsible for guiding the development of human motion tracking Azure edge and cloud services and associated SDKs. Prior to this, he was a founding member of the team that developed both HoloLens and the first Windows MR headsets.

Since joining Microsoft in 1995, Quentin has worked on numerous products, including MSN, Windows NT4 and Windows 2000 networking, Windows for Express Networks server appliances, Windows for Smart Cards, MSN/Windows Live Mobile Services, and Exchange. Before joining Microsoft, Quentin worked for Radio Free Europe/Radio Liberty in Germany. He has also worked for Best Knowledge Systems and Leeds & Northrup in New Zealand.

New Zealand born, Quentin holds bachelor's and master's degrees in electrical engineering from the University of Auckland and is an IEEE Senior Member. Quentin and his wife Lisa live in Sammamish, WA, and are getting used to being empty nesters.

Acknowledgments

Software programming is rarely a lonely journey – one of its best parts is the opportunity to learn from and with others. During my professional race, I've been blessed to work with inspiring people, mentors, and friends. Special thanks to the following people.

Georgia Makoudi for her solid debugging skills and assistance in configuring the Azure cloud. But, most importantly, for being a great friend.

Konstantinos Egkarchos for introducing me to the world of Unity cross-platform development and passionately reminding me what it is like to be a constant learner.

George Karakatsiotis for his obsession to detail and never-ending prompt to become the best version of myself.

Evangelia Schoina for being there whenever I needed a push or a break.

And my father, Panagiotis, for teaching me maths, physics, and the search for truth as a way of life.

Introduction

It's the early 1970s, and Led Zeppelin have just released their 8-minute-long Stairway to Heaven. On a European University campus, a physics student holds a shoe box and walks to a building that looks like a library. Instead of bookshelves, the building stores something weird: a thick, shiny machine called a "computer." The student, who happens to be my father, takes a seat in front of the machine and opens the shoe box. It contains multiple pieces of stiff paper with holes in it. My dad used such punch cards to write primitive software programs – his goal was to get some mathematical calculations done. One typo, and he should repunch an entire card.

Fast-forward 35 years. Information technology has become a distinct hot field of study, and I'm doing my major in computer science. Spending most of the time in front of a flat monitor, coding looks nothing like it used to. I've got rich text editors that point out my typos before I even run my programs. After a few keystrokes, I've got a fully functioning app with a graphical user interface ready, all while at the same time listening to Led Zeppelin crystal clear in my web browser.

A while ago, I was checking the news feed on my smartphone. Computer science students wear holographic headsets and project digital objects in front of their eyes. The headsets track their fingers and recognize their voice commands, allowing them to navigate the 3D virtual world without "obsolete" devices like keyboards. Even though I can't hear it, I feel they are listening to the Stairway on their tiny earphones.

What Is This Book About?

In a world where only exceptional rock music remains immutable, technology is moving so fast that it is vastly changing the way we interact with machines. Our computers become smarter and use additional sensors to understand their environment. This book will focus on a device that started a revolutionary interaction between humans and machines: the Microsoft Kinect.

Kinect is an innovative device that combines the power of multiple sensors: a video camera, a depth processor, an accelerometer, a gyroscope, and an array of microphones. By effectively streaming information from all these sensors, Kinect can sense the world in three dimensions and lay the ground for cutting-edge Artificial Intelligence applications.

In the following chapters, we'll investigate the anatomy of the Kinect device and explore the different data types coming from each sensor. Next, we'll feed the data to AI systems to detect people's silhouettes and capture the positions of human body joints. Finally, we'll see how to use this information to create interactive Augmented Reality games and, the best part, how to build our own digital personal trainer to assist with our daily fitness routine.

Who Is This Book For?

If you are reading these lines, I assume you want to learn more about creating software for that fantastic device. To take the most out of this book, you'll need an Azure Kinect camera and a strong Windows computer to write and deploy your programs.

All the example code is written in C#, so I expect you to be familiar with C# and .NET framework. You should be comfortable with the C# syntax, object-oriented programming, and basic data structures. There's no need to be a C# master, but you'll save a lot of time and googling by learning the C# basics. The graphical user interface of the examples is created in Unity3D. I have tried to keep each sample short and straightforward, so even beginners can follow. Of course, the core principles of working with Kinect data apply to any other language and framework.

PART I

Meet the Kinect

CHAPTER 1

Mixed Reality and Kinect

In the beginning, it was the punch card. In less than 100 years, the world has gone from massive, room-sized computers to tiny headsets that can project holograms and understand the world around them. We are starting our journey from the early pioneers of the science of information technology. We are going to explore how the world transitioned from primitive dumb computers to Artificial Intelligence and Mixed Reality interfaces, creating miraculous devices such as the Azure Kinect.

A Brief History of Mixed Reality

In the late 1940s, the Moore School of Electrical Engineering, University of Pennsylvania, developed the first general-purpose computer. ENIAC[1] was a gigantic machine, capable of performing ballistic calculations for the US Army. It occupied approximately 170 square meters (1800 square feet), weighed 30 tons, and contained 70,000 resistors! Input and output were accomplished by the use of punch cards, and programming was a complex task that could take weeks. The ENIAC could execute 5,000 instructions per second. Sounds impressive? It was. With today's standards, though, an iPhone 6 (released 2014) could execute 25 billion instructions per second[2]! Figure 1-1 shows how an ENIAC filled a whole room.

---

[1] ENIAC: Electronic Numerical Integrator and Computer
[2] That's 5,000 versus 25,000,000,000.

© Vangos Pterneas 2022
V. Pterneas, *Mastering the Microsoft Kinect*, https://doi.org/10.1007/978-1-4842-8070-6_1

Figure 1-1. *ENIAC – the first electronic, Turing complete computer*

Computers like ENIAC were not supposed to be used by the public, requiring a lot of trained programmers to operate. It would take three decades for computers to become small enough to be considered "personal." With smaller sizes came new means of interaction: the keyboard, an invention of the 19th century, allowed operators to type their commands directly instead of using paper cards.

But computer users needed more immediate control. The first mouse was invented in 1964 by Douglas Engelbart,[3] allowing computer operators to point and select graphical elements on the screen. The mouse was developed further in the 1970s and 1980s, becoming the most mainstream computer input device – reigning the industry until today. Graphical user interfaces are partially what made computers mainstream and accessible to people without technical programming knowledge.

---

[3] Fun fact: The first mouse consisted of a wooden shell, a circuit board, and two perpendicular metal wheels.

Another groundbreaking invention of the 1960s is the touchscreen. The touchscreen allows even more natural interaction between the operator and the computer. Instead of using additional hardware to point to screen elements, a touchscreen enables direct interaction with the computer application. Touchscreens evolved over the years, and with the rapid expansion of mobile devices, they became part of our everyday lives. Nowadays, smartphones and tablets are replacing a lot of tasks humanity had been used to doing with personal computers.

So what's next?

Natural User Interfaces

Regardless of the real breakthroughs in human-computer communication, science fiction has always been a step ahead of the actual science. Remember Scotty in Star Trek IV attempting to speak to a Macintosh? It was pretty common for sci-fi heroes to use their gestures and voice to interact with computers, leaving ordinary people like us wondering whether those futuristic interfaces would sometime be available.

In 2009, Microsoft took a giant leap and introduced the first affordable device that was capable of doing precisely that. The device was codenamed "Project Natal" and, in 2010, was released under the name "Kinect" as an accessory for the XBOX 360 gaming console. The accessory could recognize the body parts of the people and could understand their voice as they were speaking. This way, players could interact with the console without using a controller! Kinect earned the Guinness World Record for the fastest-selling consumer electronics device of all time in 2010. It wasn't until 2017 that Nintendo Switch dethroned Kinect.

Figure 1-2. *Kinect version 1 for XBOX 360 (2010)*

Soon enough, tinkerers and hackers around the world started connecting the Kinect device to their computers, trying to access its features. Microsoft followed and, in 2011, released the first Kinect Software Development Kit for Windows operating systems. For the first time, developers had access to body-tracking and voice-recognition technology that was only available in sci-fi.

Two years later, Microsoft introduced the successor of the XBOX 360 console: XBOX ONE. Along with XBOX ONE came the second version of the successful Kinect device.

Figure 1-3. *Kinect version 2 for XBOX ONE (2014)*

Kinect version 2 had much better hardware specifications than Kinect version 1, resulting in higher body-tracking accuracy. Yet the gaming industry turned its back to the new motion controller. Hardcore gamers felt that their hard-earned XP and hundreds of gaming hours with the precision controllers wouldn't matter any longer. As a result, no significant games were developed; thus, fewer and fewer gamers used the device. However, Kinect found fruitful ground in nongaming industries. Companies started to realize its potential in various fields, including fitness, entertainment, and even health care. Business applications soon bypassed games, and a new possibility seemed to arise.

Microsoft stopped providing updates to the software and moved on with different projects.

And then, Mixed Reality entered our lives.

In 2016, Microsoft unveiled a head-mounted display with a small computer unit and various sensors attached. The device could sense the world around it, detect surfaces, and project holograms in front of the human eyes. People wearing these smart glasses could see virtual objects overlaid in the real world. The headset was named "HoloLens," and the coexistence of digital and physical objects was called "Mixed Reality."

HoloLens also featured Cortana, a personal assistant that can understand voice commands and respond to user's questions. Users could hear the virtual assistant through built-in headphones and touch the holograms with their fingers. Moreover, HoloLens could download data from the cloud, process them, and enhance its intelligence further.

From a business point of view, HoloLens had a higher-end target market: businesses.

Figure 1-4. *The first version of Microsoft HoloLens (2016)*

Following the success of HoloLens in nongaming industries, Microsoft soon realized that Kinect could be much more than gaming peripheral. Instead of controlling a game, Kinect could be a means to **understand** the world and its surroundings. Human body tracking, voice recognition, and motion analysis are only a small part of what Kinect can achieve. Such capabilities have way more practical applications than controlling a virtual character.

Microsoft took everyone by surprise and announced a brand-new, yet familiar, device in its Build 2018 conference: Project Kinect for Azure. The next generation of Kinect was alive and started shipping in July 2019.

Figure 1-5. *Kinect for Azure (2019)*

Project Kinect for Azure was born as a direct offspring of HoloLens. Most of the HoloLens hardware components (such as the Time-of-Flight depth sensor) are present in the Azure Kinect device too. Why not use HoloLens, instead, then? Three reasons:

1. The primary goal of HoloLens is, well, hologram projection and spatial understanding. On the other hand, Kinect is a computer accessory.

2. HoloLens is attached to the head of the user. Kinect (usually) remains on a stable point, thus accommodating different use-case scenarios.

3. HoloLens is a stand-alone device with limited hardware specifications. Kinect is using the power of a personal computer. That's a fundamental benefit compared to HoloLens because using the extra power of a PC, Kinect can increase its range and efficiency.

If the word "Azure" sounds misleading to you, we are going to explain more in the next sections. *Hint: The sensor does not require an Internet connection to run.*

Microsoft armed the new Kinect device with a couple of powerful software development kits: a Sensor SDK and a Body Tracking SDK. The SDKs allow developers to access the streams of the device and use its AI features right out of the box.

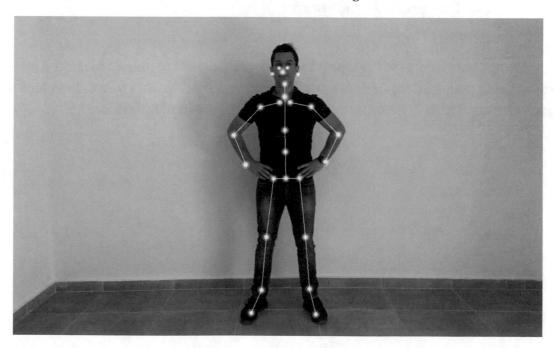

Figure 1-6. *Human body tracking with the Azure Kinect sensor*

How is all this functionality even possible? To start, let's take a close look at the hardware. In the next chapter, I am also going to introduce you to the software.

Kinect Sensor Anatomy

In our modern world, "magic" is called "science." Having seen what the Kinect can do, it's time to understand how this miraculous piece of hardware works. Let's start by breaking it down to its discrete parts.

What if I told you that the Azure Kinect device is not a single camera? It is, actually, a container of separate hardware components, assembled into one unit. Most of these components are derived, in the same or different form, from HoloLens. Each component performs a particular function. The "Kinect bundle" includes

- 12MP RGB video camera

- 1MP depth sensor

- Seven-microphone array

- IMU (accelerometer and gyroscope)

- External sync pins

The software combines the input of all these components to provide magical capabilities: body tracking, point clouds, voice recognition, etc. Let's take a closer look at each element. Figure 1-7 illustrates where every hardware module is located.[4]

---

[4] If you are wondering how I removed the plastic case, keep in mind that Kinect is primarily targeting tinkerers. The Kinect Development Kit comes with an Allen wrench to unscrew the pins by yourself. This is especially useful if you are building custom installations and you need to adjust the hardware accordingly.

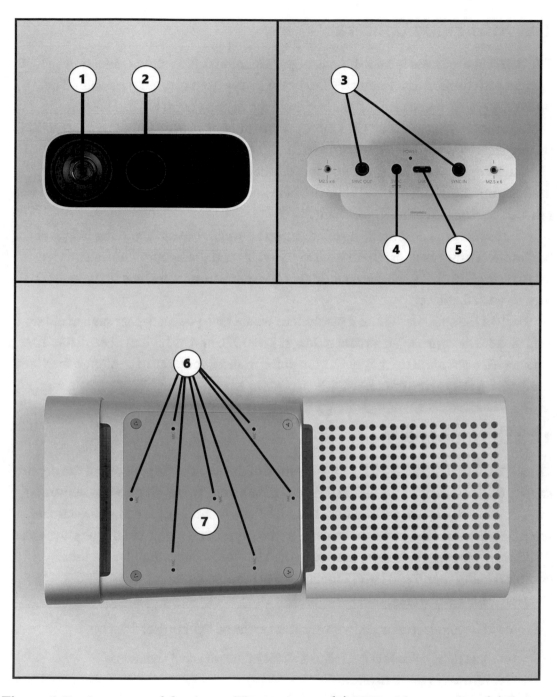

Figure 1-7. *Anatomy of the Azure Kinect sensor: (1) RGB video camera, (2) ToF depth sensor, (3) external synchronization pins, (4) power cable port, (5) USB-C cable port, (6) microphone array, (7) inertial measurement unit*

The RGB Video Camera

The RGB video camera is a traditional, high-resolution rolling shutter sensor. The RGB camera can operate just like any USB webcam you've used on your computer. The operating system can use the camera without the development kit.

Like most webcams, the RGB Kinect camera provides a 2D colored representation of the physical world.

Unlike most webcams, the RGB Kinect camera supports six different operating modes. You, the developer, can choose which mode to operate. The resolution and frame rate can be adjusted programmatically.

The aspect ratio describes the relationship between the width and the height of the frame. It's the result of the division of the width and the height. The field of view (FOV) is that part of the physical world that is visible through the lens of the camera. It's measured in degrees.

Each of the supported Kinect resolutions would give you an aspect ratio of either 16:9 or 4:3. The camera can stream as low as 1280×720 and as high as 3840×2160. That is a native 4K resolution! In Chapter 4, I am going to show you how to configure the video camera and stream the frames.

The Depth Sensor

The RGB camera provides a 2D representation of the world. With the use of the depth sensor, the 2D view is expanded to the third dimension. This is all possible because of the Time-of-Flight (ToF) technology. Time-of-Flight technology is a highly accurate method of measuring the distance between the sensor and a point in the physical space.

Various signal types can be used with the Time-of-Flight principle, the most common being sound and light. Kinect is using infrared light beams.

Here's how ToF works:

- The depth sensor emits a very short infrared light pulse.

- The light pulse is reflected in a point in the physical space and returns to the sensor.

- Each pixel of the sensor measures the return time of that pulse.

- The longer it took the pulse to return, the bigger the distance!

To distinguish between color and depth, keep the following in mind: a color point is a mix of red, green, and blue values. A depth point is, simply, a **distance** value. The depth camera has no information about colors! In the following, I have visualized the depth stream by assigning each distance a different color value.

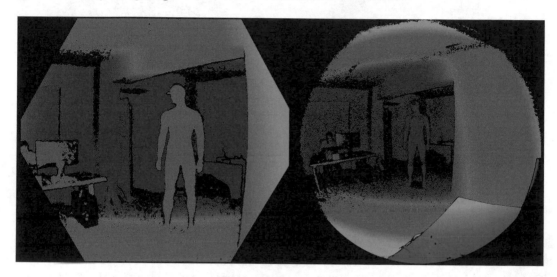

Figure 1-8. *Narrow (left) and wide (right) depth field of views*

As you noticed in Figure 1-8, Kinect can operate in one of two modes: narrow field of view (NFOV) and wide field of view (WFOV). The narrow FOV has a resolution of either 320×288 or 640×576. The wide FOV has a resolution of either 512×512 or 1024×1024. As you can see, the wide FOV can capture a much bigger picture of the environment. However, NFOV sees out to approximately 6 meters (20 feet), while WFOV only sees out to about 3 meters (10 feet). That's a reasonable energy trade-off: long range vs. wide view.

Caution   Higher resolutions come at a higher performance overhead. Selecting the proper configuration is critical for the success of your application. Does your application need to see a big or a small part of the world? Is a small number of frames acceptable as a performance trade-off? These are all questions you need to answer before typing any code.

Just like the color field of view, the depth field of view can also be specified programmatically.

Figure 1-9 puts the color and depth fields of view in perspective, allowing you to understand the overlap between them.

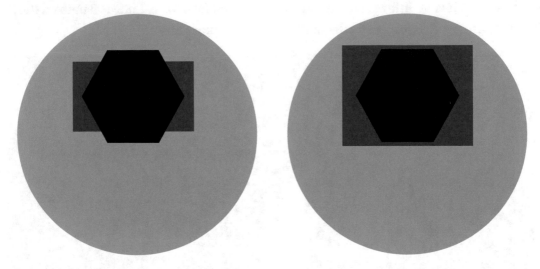

Figure 1-9. *Azure Kinect fields of view. The circle represents the depth WFOV, the hexagon represents the depth NFOV, and the rectangle represents the RGB FOV. On the left, the RGB view has a 16:9 aspect ratio, while on the right, it has a 4:3 aspect ratio*

Also notice how the frames are shaped: the RGB color frame is a traditional rectangle. The depth NFOV is also a rectangle, but it's only filled as a hexagon. The rest of the pixels are black. Same thing applies to the WFOV; only this one is circular. It's counterintuitive, but each frame type sees a slightly different area of the world. As you would expect, when the depth sensor operates in narrow mode, it has a much better overlap with the 4:3 RGB resolution than the 16:9 one. The reason is simple: more common points are visible to the two cameras when the height of the RGB sensor is bigger.

In Chapter 8, we'll see how to map between the RGB and the depth streams and explore the relationships between them.

Figures 1-10 and 1-11 make it easier to grasp the concept of the concurrent fields of view.

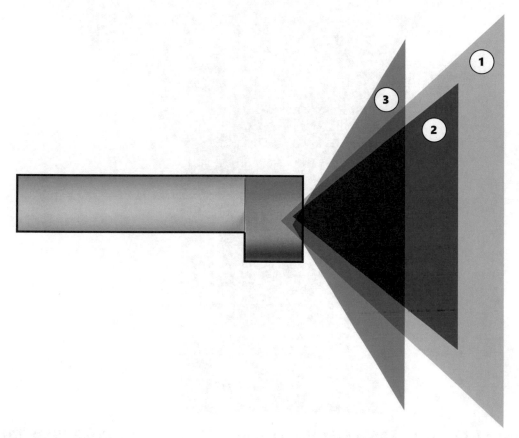

Figure 1-10. *Azure Kinect field of view (side). (1) RGB FOV, (2) depth NFOV, (3) depth WFOV*

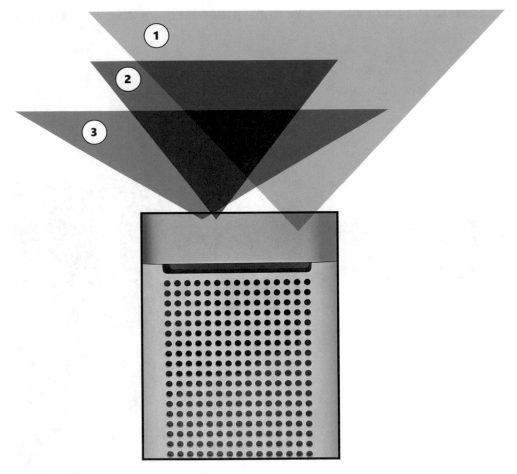

Figure 1-11. *Azure Kinect field of view (top). (1) RGB FOV, (2) depth NFOV, (3) depth WFOV*

The Microphone Arrays

Kinect is also equipped with seven microphones, positioned at the top of the device. The layout of the microphone array allows Kinect to filter your voice and eliminate noise as much as possible.

When examining a microphone, we mostly care about its sensitivity. The sensitivity of a microphone is a negative number specifying the amount of output for a given input. The closer that number to zero, the greater the signal of the microphone.

Kinect microphones have a sensitivity value of -22 sBFS. Considering that typical values for most condenser mics range from -40 to -30, Kinect is doing pretty good. The device will do its best to filter and understand your voice as much as possible.

The IMU (Accelerometer and Gyroscope)

Similar to a typical smartphone, Kinect also includes an accelerometer and a gyroscope.

The accelerometer is used to detect the orientation of the device relative to the surface of the Earth. The gyroscope is used to measure rotational changes of the device around the three axes of motion (X, Y, Z). The accelerometer is measuring the linear velocity when the device is stationary. On the other hand, the gyroscope is unaffected by the acceleration of the device.

In Chapter 7, we'll see how to detect the rotation of the device around the horizontal (X), vertical (Y), and depth (Z) axes.

Spec-wise, the accelerometer and gyroscope are simultaneously sampled at 1.6 kHz. The samples are reported to the host at 208 Hz.

The combination of the accelerometer and the gyroscope is also referred to as the "inertial measurement unit" or "IMU."

The External Sync Pins

Lastly, Kinect includes a couple of 3.5-mm external synchronization ports: Sync in and Sync out. You can use these tiny pins to connect multiple Kinect devices on the same computer. Upon joining the devices, the software can operate them at the same time, providing accurately timed samples.

Using two or more Kinect devices on the same computer could have a lot of potential applications, such as

- Scanning objects simultaneously from multiple angles

- Covering large areas

- Combining more frames to get smoother results (depth, skeleton)

- Performing photogrammetry

Enhancing Kinect with Azure

So far, we have been using the term "Azure Kinect" without having clarified why it was named this way. After all, Azure is the registered trademark of the popular Microsoft cloud computing platform. Consequently, most people would rightly assume that the device requires an Internet connection and a cloud subscription. That is not true, though.

Kinect is a stand-alone device, and its core software APIs (sensor and body tracking) run offline. No Internet connection is required, and no data is stored on the cloud. Developers do not even need an Azure subscription. If you are familiar with the older Kinect for XBOX devices, the color, depth, and skeleton data are also provided out of the box via the offline SDKs.

But offline SDKs only go far. Azure is the next level, providing unlimited possibilities for your applications. The Azure platform is a vast provider of advanced Machine Learning and Artificial Intelligence algorithms. Accessing those algorithms via a web API would give your applications new superpowers.

Imagine streaming the RGB and depth data to the cloud, while a remote Machine Learning component is recognizing objects and shapes. Or imagine providing the microphone input to a cloud service, and the service recognizes the voice and responds to commands – just like Cortana. In Chapters 15 and 16, we are going to tap into the Azure Cognitive Services platform and develop our own cloud AI application.

It's now clear why Kinect was designed with cloud in mind, not just the Microsoft Azure cloud, but any cloud provider!

Key Points

In the first chapter, we took a short history tour of the fascinating world of Mixed Reality. We explored the human-computer interaction and have seen how this evolved. From command-line to graphical interfaces, to touch screens, to holograms, it's been a long journey.

The Azure Kinect device is a combination of different hardware components: a Time-of-Flight depth sensor, an RGB video camera, an array of seven microphones, and an inertial measurement unit with an accelerometer and a gyroscope. Kinect is feeding the input of all these components to its AI software and produces jaw-dropping results, such as body tracking, voice recognition, and 3D point clouds.

Kinect can enhance its built-in capabilities by connecting to the Microsoft Azure cloud platform and utilizing its remote Machine Learning features.

So unbox your sensor and connect it to your computer. In the next chapter, we are going to set up our development environment and start writing code for the Kinect device.

CHAPTER 2

The Developer Toolbox

We introduced the amazing Kinect hardware in Chapter 1. As a next step, we are going to explore how you, the developer, can utilize this hardware into your software. The Kinect device includes different hardware modules for accomplishing various tasks. In this chapter, we are going to set up the development environment and get our hands dirty. But most importantly, you will learn how to make the right decisions and balance between exceptional quality and maximum performance.

Overview of the Microsoft Azure SDK

As we mentioned in Chapter 1, Kinect is not a single device, but rather a bundle of several components. As it's clear from their names, the video camera is capturing color information, while the depth camera is capturing distances. The microphones are listening for audio. The accelerometer and gyroscope are measuring acceleration and rotation, respectively. We need a way to access all this information programmatically.

The Azure Kinect Software Development Kit (SDK) is a set of programming interfaces that acquire the input from all these hardware modules and expresses it in the form of code. You can think of the SDK as your middleman for accessing each component!

Let's take the depth sensor as an example. The depth sensor is capturing a frame of distances. The SDK is expressing the data as an array of integer values and allows us to visualize them as a 3D point cloud.

Remember that Kinect is still an external peripheral, without a dedicated processing unit. As a result, we need to connect it to a computer. Kinect senses the physical world and streams data. The computer receives and processes that data.

To help developers with Kinect data processing, Microsoft has provided two separate development kits: the Sensor SDK and the Body Tracking SDK. Additionally, the Azure cloud platform offers more online tools. For now, we'll focus on the two essential SDKs we can use without an Internet connection.

So plug your Kinect device into your computer and follow along.

© Vangos Pterneas 2022
V. Pterneas, *Mastering the Microsoft Kinect*, https://doi.org/10.1007/978-1-4842-8070-6_2

Azure Kinect Sensor SDK

The Sensor SDK allows us to access the raw data streams, which is the bare minimum you need to write a simple Kinect application:

- RGB color data

- Depth data

- Audio data

- Acceleration measurement

- Rotation measurement

Microsoft open-sourced the Sensor SDK, and it's hosted on GitHub. The community is free to build the SDK from scratch, modify the code, and even contribute to the public repository.[1] The documentation is available online too.[2]

Of course, we do not need to build the whole project ourselves, as Microsoft is providing pre-built binaries for Windows and Linux, which correspond to the latest stable release.[3]

You read this right: Following Microsoft's commitment to open-source, the Sensor SDK is available for both Windows and Linux operating systems. As a developer, you can reach a wider audience and ship your applications using the operating system of your choice. Speaking of that, let's see what exactly you need to run the SDK on your computer.

Sensor SDK System Requirements

Microsoft has set the minimum hardware specifications for accessing the raw streams programmatically, as shown in Table 2-1.

---

[1] Sensor SDK source code: `https://github.com/Microsoft/Azure-Kinect-Sensor-SDK`

[2] Sensor SDK documentation: `https://microsoft.github.io/Azure-Kinect-Sensor-SDK/`

[3] Sensor SDK binaries: `https://docs.microsoft.com/en-us/azure/kinect-dk/sensor-sdk-download`

Table 2-1. *Azure Kinect Sensor SDK minimum system requirements*

Component	Requirement
Processor (CPU)	7th generation Intel Core i3 (Dual-Core 2.4 GHz)
Graphics card (GPU)	Intel HD Graphics 620
RAM	4GB
Ports	One dedicated USB 3 port
Operating system	Windows 10 version 1803 (x64) or Ubuntu Linux 18.04 (x64)

As you may have noticed, Table 2-1 describes a relatively moderate computer. However, here is the caveat: since the Sensor Development Kit is supposed to run on a wide range of platforms, performance differs according to a variety of factors, the most important of which is the graphics card drivers, the operating system, as well as the sensor configuration used in the application.

Long story short, the better the specs of your computer, the higher the performance will be. In the upcoming chapters, we are going to identify rules of thumb and best practices to optimize your Kinect applications for the target environment. Continuous testing and experimentation are, obviously, critical – you should never assume that a program running on a single computer would have identical behavior on a different one.

Thankfully, the Azure Kinect Sensor SDK includes a tool that helps us see the available configurations and visualize the streams accordingly.

The Kinect Viewer

The Azure Kinect Viewer is the first application you should run upon downloading and installing the Sensor SDK. You can find the Viewer in your Start menu, or under the Program Files entry:

```
C:\Program Files\Azure Kinect SDK v1.4.0\tools
```

The Azure Kinect Viewer provides a holistic overview of the available streams. Figure 2-1 displays what my Kinect is seeing and hearing right now.

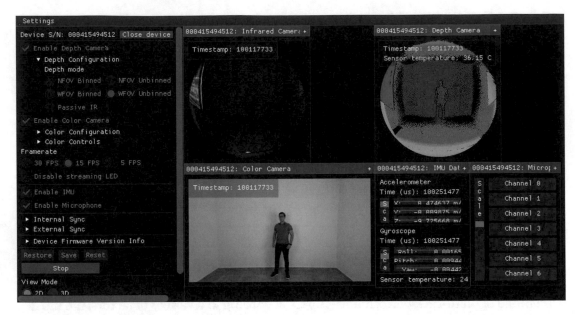

Figure 2-1. *The Azure Kinect Viewer in action. On the left, find the available controls. On the right, find the available visualizations: infrared, depth, color, acceleration, rotation, and audio*

On the left-hand sidebar, you'll notice the available configurations. Remember when we said that the depth camera could provide either a narrow or a wide field of view? Here is where you can select which one to see. Similarly, you can switch between the available color resolutions and aspect ratios. Moreover, the Viewer is showing the infrared view, the audio input, as well as the device acceleration and rotation.

If you have more than one Kinect device connected, the Viewer identifies their serial numbers and allows you to switch between them,[4] as shown in Figure 2-2.

---

[4] Along with the live camera feed, the Azure Kinect Viewer supports video playback from Matroska video files (MKV). There is a different utility, called k4arecorder.exe, which allows you to record the streams. This is out of the scope of the book but may be handy if you need to process Kinect data without accessing a physical Kinect device. The recorder tool is located in the same folder to the Azure Kinect Viewer.

Figure 2-2. *The connected Azure Kinect devices*

Let's take a closer look at the visualized streams. We shall start with the depth stream. As you already know, depth frames consist of nothing but a series of distance, measured in millimeters.[5] How could we visualize a set of distance values? Simple: we assign a color range to a distance range. The Kinect Viewer is using shades of blue for close-distance points, shades of green for mid-range points, and shades of red for faraway points. Black colors indicate that the depth of that particular point could not be identified. We'll see the actual code in Chapter 5.

Figure 2-3 shows the depth visualization of the narrow field of view (NFOV) and the wide field of view (WFOV).

---

[5] If you are not using the Metric system, the Appendix of this book provides some handful conversion formulas. The Kinect SDK is using meters, millimeters, and degrees Celsius instead of feet, inches, and degrees Fahrenheit.

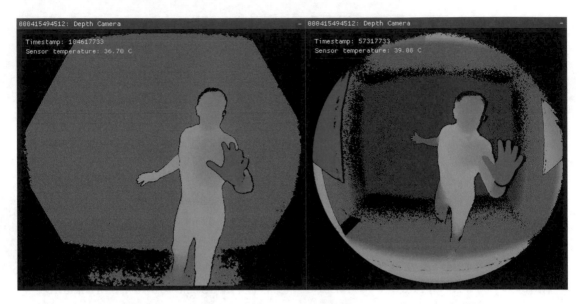

Figure 2-3. *Depth visualization. NFOV (left) and WFOV (right)*

Along with the depth map, the Viewer is also demonstrating the active brightness infrared (IR) image, as displayed in Figure 2-4. The active brightness IR reading is similar to the depth view, but its pixels are drawn in shades of gray. Each gray value is proportional to the amount of light returned from the physical scene.

Figure 2-4. *The clean infrared reading. Each pixel is assigned a shade of gray, from white to black*

The next Kinect Viewer visualization is the RGB video camera reading. Based on the configuration settings you applied on the sidebar, you'll see the corresponding color image. Figure 2-5 shows a color frame with a 16:9 aspect ratio (1920×1080 resolution), while Figure 2-6 shows a color frame with a 4:3 aspect ratio and a 4K resolution.

Figure 2-5. *RGB color frame with an aspect ratio of 16:9*

Figure 2-6. *RGB color frame with an aspect ratio of 4:3. Notice how much vertical space is available!*

Let's move on to some seemingly weirder visuals. The IMU Data panel shows real-time acceleration and rotation measurements. Acceleration is measured in meters per second squared, while rotation is measured in radians per second. You can move and rotate your Kinect device to see these readings change. To adjust the scale of the graph in the Kinect Viewer app, simply use the vertical sliders, as shown in Figure 2-7.

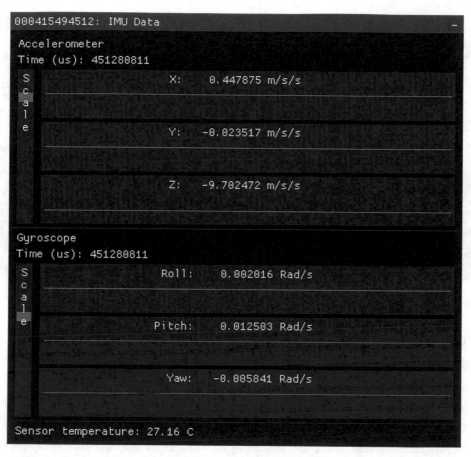

Figure 2-7. *The accelerometer and gyroscope readings*

Last but not least, the Kinect Viewer is displaying the audio input from its seven microphones. Here is a simple way to test this: get close to your Kinect and speak in various tones. The audio waveform would appear in the Microphone Data panel. Notice that the waveform is slightly different on every microphone due to their spatial positions (Figure 2-8).

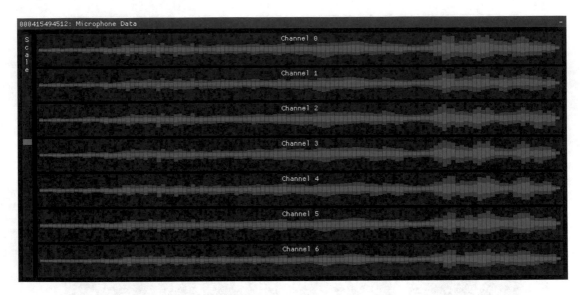

Figure 2-8. *The audio captured by each of the seven microphones*

By that, you have a good understanding of the input data Kinect is capturing in real time. Each hardware component is responsible for a single type of information (color, depth, acceleration, rotation, audio). We are calling these values "raw data." It's exactly this combination of different raw data types that produces impressive results.

Get back to the Azure Kinect Viewer and click the "3D" button. There will be displayed one extra panel that's not visible by default: the Point Cloud view (Figure 2-9). The Point Cloud Viewer combines the input of the depth and video cameras and produces a 3D representation of the physical world. Use your mouse to rotate the view and watch your room in 3D.

Figure 2-9. *The colorized 3D point cloud viewer*

How is that even possible? Based on our understanding of the hardware modules, here is what's happening:

- The Azure Kinect SDK acquires the depth and video frames.

- The software then aligns the two frames. As a result, each depth point has a corresponding color point.

- The Viewer is drawing small cubes with a size of 2 pixels.

- Based on its depth distance, each cube is relatively positioned closer to or farther from the point of view.

- Each cube is colored according to its RGB values.

Not so complicated, right? In Chapter 8, you'll learn how to access the Kinect cameras and transform between the 2D and the 3D space.

Azure Kinect Body Tracking SDK

Creating 3D representations of the world is only one of the Azure Kinect possibilities. Combining the Azure Kinect streams can produce significantly more advanced results. Meet the Body Tracking SDK, a software kit that allows you to detect human bodies and track the positions of 32 points. These points can be skeletal joints, such as shoulders, elbows, and knees, or landmarks, such as ears, eyes, and nose.

Simple camera transformations alone are not capable of accomplishing such a demanding and fuzzy task – we need bigger brains. You may be familiar with the cutting-edge Artificial Intelligence (AI) and Machine Learning (ML) breakthroughs. Artificial Intelligence is a mathematical-based way of making computers carry out scenarios we consider "smart" and "complicated." Machine Learning is an application of Artificial Intelligence that's using annotated data to train the machines and let them learn the way humans do.

To put it simply, if we train a machine with thousands of images of the human eye, then computers will be able to recognize the eyes in new photos.

Microsoft has trained an AI system to segment the human body and recognize its joints. Similar to the point cloud algorithm, this system is combining the information of the color and depth frames. Only this time, the process is not trivial at all. We cannot easily create a step-by-step recipe to distinguish between elbows and shoulders – this is the job of AI. You don't need to know anything about AI and ML to use the SDK, though. All the heavy lifting has been done for us. The Body Tracking SDK is capturing and exposing the skeletal information in a way we can access and manage.

Body Tracking SDK System Requirements

Naturally, AI and ML are resource intensive, and thus, their demands in processing power tend to be very high. Machine Learning algorithms are doing tremendous amounts of calculations per second, especially matrix multiplications. The CPU itself is not optimized to doing that many calculations. As a result, we are shifting this burden to the GPU! The GPU is already optimized for accomplishing millions of computations at a fraction of a second. You have seen this happening when you play games with realistic 3D graphics.

Table 2-2 shows the system requirements of the Azure Kinect Body Tracking SDK.

Table 2-2. *Azure Kinect Body Tracking SDK minimum system requirements*

Component	Requirement
Processor (CPU)	7th generation Intel Core i5 (Quad-Core 2.4 GHz)
Graphics card (GPU)	NVIDIA GeForce GTX 1050 or equivalent
RAM	4GB
Ports	One dedicated USB 3 port
Operating system	Windows 10 version 1803 (x64) or Ubuntu Linux 18.04 (x64)

The main difference with the Sensor SDK is the GPU required. The initial versions of the Azure Kinect Body Tracking SDK required an NVIDIA GTX 1070 or better and only supported NVIDIA cards.[6] More recent updates, though, removed that barrier: not only did Microsoft add compatibility with lower-end cards, but they also supported additional manufacturers, including AMD and Intel.

So here comes the first decision you will need to make: What kind of computer are you going to use? Sure, as a developer, chances are you have a pretty good machine. What about your users and customers, though? Suggesting them to purchase a super-expensive laptop may not be an option, after all. To answer this dilemma, think whether you'll need body-tracking functionality, which is significantly impacting the cost of the computer. If you are, instead, going to use the Kinect to simply process some depth data or transmit voice to the cloud, then you don't need a high-end computer.

---

[6] The first versions of the Azure Kinect neural engine required the CUDA toolkit, which is only available on NVIDIA graphics cards. Newer versions are using DirectML, instead, which is compatible with most vendors.

The Kinect Body Tracking Viewer

The Azure Kinect Body Tracking SDK comes with its Viewer application as well. You can search for it in your Start menu or locate it under

```
C:\Program Files\Azure Kinect Body Tracking SDK\tools
```

Upon launching the Body Tracking Viewer, you should see a 3D depth view with highlighted human bodies and joints. Move around and check how Kinect is tracking your skeleton. Chapter 6 is dedicated to the Azure Kinect Body Tracking capabilities.

Figure 2-10. *Azure Kinect human body segmentation and joint tracking (default front view)*

Use your mouse to rotate the 3D view and look at your pose in the front, side, and even overhead planes of motion.

Figure 2-11. *Azure Kinect human body segmentation and joint tracking (overhead view)[7]*

The Azure Kinect Viewer tools are essential during more complex development phases. It's highly recommended to use them as reference points to ensure your apps behave properly.

Setting Up the Development Environment

Since you now have both SDKs installed, it's time to configure your development environment. As we've already mentioned, the Azure Kinect SDKs run on Windows and Ubuntu Linux machines.[8] Microsoft officially supports the following programming languages:

- C

- C++

---

[7] Fun fact: When I was showcasing Kinect's overhead view, people could not understand how a front-facing sensor could track the joints in three dimensions. Some of them unconsciously looked at the ceiling to ensure I had not placed a second Kinect device there!

[8] Additionally, if you are a fan of portable ARM boards, Jetson Nano and Jetson TX2 are supported.

- C#

- Python

From my seven-year-old experience developing Kinect applications, most developers are using Kinect to create interactive applications with stunning visuals and 3D content. That's the reason I have chosen to focus on the C# programming language and the Unity3D engine.

Keep in mind that the core principles we'll describe in this book apply to every programming language. Focus on understanding the process behind every technical decision. Doing so will allow you to easily port your code to different platforms and programming languages if necessary.

Unity3D and Visual Studio

Unity3D is a game and application development engine. Unity3D allows us to design our user interface (either 2D or 3D) using a simple, visual, drag-and-drop editor. One of its primary strengths is rapid prototyping and experimentation, especially for new Kinect developers.

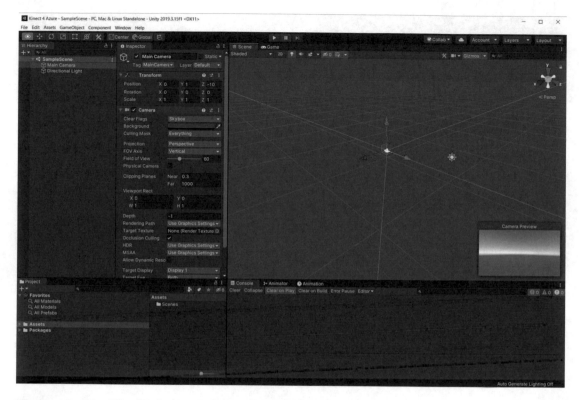

Figure 2-12. *The Unity3D Editor window*

Unity3D allows us to create graphical objects and specify their characteristics and properties. To interact with the virtual objects and update their behavior, we need to assign them a C# script. There is no more convenient way to write and debug C# code than Visual Studio.

Visual Studio is an Integrated Development Environment (IDE) developed and maintained by Microsoft. You can download Visual Studio Community for free[9] or install it as part of your Unity3D installation package.[10]

---

[9] Download Visual Studio Community 2022 or 2019: `https://visualstudio.microsoft.com/`

[10] Download Unity3D with Visual Studio Community: `https://store.unity.com/`

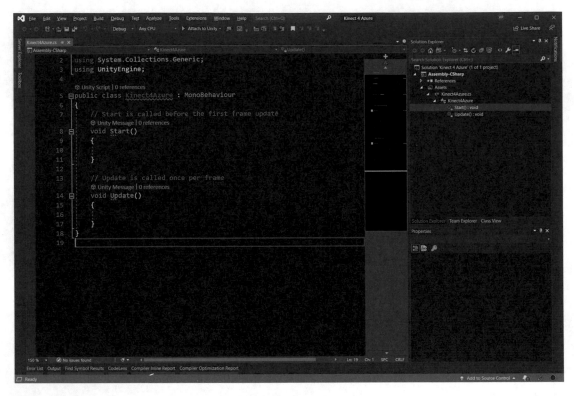

Figure 2-13. *Visual Studio 2019 with a simple C# file open*

Since you are reading this book, I assume you are already familiar with Unity3D and C# development. In case you are a veteran programmer with no Unity experience or a newbie to Unity, head to the official tutorials and guides.[11] You'll be able to grasp the main ideas and jump to writing code very quickly. The examples in this book are going to be very thorough; however, we are not going to cover the basic aspects of C# programming or the fundamentals of the Unity Engine.

---

[11] Unity3D tutorials and getting-started guides: `https://unity.com/learn`

Bringing It All Together

Throughout this book, I'll be using Windows 10 because the Body Tracking SDK is not yet officially available for Unity3D on Linux. In terms of Unity, I'll be using the latest Unity3D LTS version[12] with Visual Studio Community 2019 (you can use 2022 – it doesn't really matter). My developer setup looks like this:

- Windows 10 version 1909 (x64)

- Unity3D 2019 LTS

- Visual Studio 2019 Community

- Azure Kinect Sensor SDK version 1.4.0

- Azure Kinect Body Tracking SDK version 1.0.1

We now have the required tools in our belt. As a next step, we need to import the Azure Kinect SDK in Unity3D and start writing some magic. Fasten your seatbelt and get ready for our first coding adventure in Chapter 3!

Key Points

In the second chapter, we explored how the physical hardware components of the Azure Kinect can feed the software with the corresponding data.

Microsoft is providing two offline software development kits: the Azure Kinect Sensor SDK and the Azure Kinect Body Tracking SDK. The first one is responsible for capturing and streaming raw data, such as color, depth, audio, acceleration, and rotation. The other is feeding the raw color and depth data to its Artificial Intelligence and Machine Learning algorithms to track the human body and joints. Such combinations of multiple Kinect streams can produce jaw-dropping results, such as body tracking, voice recognition, and 3D point clouds.

Kinect can also enhance its built-in capabilities by communicating with the Microsoft Azure cloud platform and utilizing its remote Machine Learning features.

---

[12] LTS stands for "long-term support." LTS versions of Unity3D are receiving official updates for three years. They are much more stable and, thus, strongly recommended for commercial products.

The Microsoft Kinect SDKs are providing C, C++, C#, and Python programming interfaces. For the needs of this book, we'll be using the C# programming language with the Unity3D engine and the Visual Studio code editor. The primary concepts we'll explore here apply to every other programming language and platform, though.

So unbox your sensor and connect it to your computer. In the next chapter, we are going to write some C# code to configure the sensor programmatically.

PART II

The Basics

CHAPTER 3

Configuring the Device

It's, finally, time to get our hands dirty and write some code to program the Kinect device. No matter how old I get, the enthusiasm of coding for such an exciting technology resembles the unique feeling of the first "Hello World" program I've ever written.

Adding the Kinect SDKs in Unity3D

If you've followed my lead, you've set up your developer toolbox and installed Unity3D and Visual Studio on your Windows 10 computer. You have also downloaded the Azure Kinect Sensor SDK and the Azure Kinect Body Tracking SDK.

Launch Unity3D and create a new project. Under your Assets root folder, create a folder named Plugins. The Plugins folder has a reserved name that informs Unity where the project binaries will reside. Also, organize your project structure by adding some more folders for your scenes, scripts, and prefabs. Figure 3-1 shows my Unity project structure.

© Vangos Pterneas 2022
V. Pterneas, *Mastering the Microsoft Kinect*, https://doi.org/10.1007/978-1-4842-8070-6_3

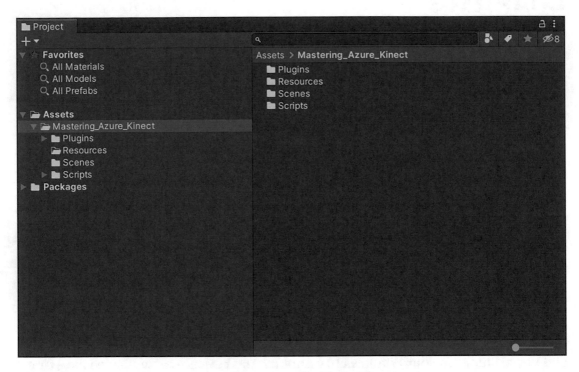

Figure 3-1. *Azure Kinect project structure in Unity3D*

Next, we are going to locate and acquire the SDK binaries. Unity3D supports two types of binaries: native C++ binaries and managed C# binaries.

The Azure Kinect Binaries

The native C++ binaries provide low-level interactivity with the device, while the C# dependencies wrap and expose the native functionality in managed code. Inside your Plugins folder, create a new folder named x86_64. The C# binaries should be pasted directly inside the Plugins folder, while the C++ binaries should be placed inside the x86_64 folder. To download the files, we'll use NuGet, the built-in package manager of Visual Studio.

1. In the Unity menu, launch Visual Studio by selecting
   Assets ➤ Open C# Project

2. In the Visual Studio menu, select Tools ➤ NuGet Package
   Manager ➤ Package Manager Console

3. Type the following command to download the Sensor SDK:
   `Install-Package Microsoft.Azure.Kinect.Sensor`
   Wait until the binaries are successfully downloaded. Accept the
   license terms, if prompted to do so.

4. Go to the official Microsoft website to download and install the
   (separate) Body Tracking SDK:
   `https://docs.microsoft.com/en-us/azure/kinect-dk/body-`
   `sdk-download`

Upon completion of the preceding actions, the `Packages` folder should be populated
with the Kinect Sensor SDK dependencies. The `Packages` folder is automatically created
for you next to your `Assets` folder – but outside your Unity project. Moreover, the Body
Tracking binaries would be under the installation location of the Body Tracking SDK. On
my machine, it's `C:\Program Files\Azure Kinect Body Tracking SDK`.

We have a ton of binaries in multiple locations. For Unity to "see" all these binaries,
we need to copy and paste them into the Unity-specific plug-in directories. Stay with me
here since this is a task you'll need to do once per project.

Managed C# Binaries

We'll copy the C# managed binaries first under the `Plugins` folder. Along with the
binaries, we are also going to copy their XML documentation files, so we can have
inline documentation in Visual Studio. Look for the following folders and copy the files
mentioned in the bullets.[1]

`packages\Microsoft.Azure.Kinect.Sensor.1.4.1\lib\netstandard2.0\`

- Microsoft.Azure.Kinect.Sensor.dll

- Microsoft.Azure.Kinect.Sensor.xml

- Microsoft.Azure.Kinect.BodyTracking.xml

   `packages\System.Buffers.4.4.0\lib\netstandard2.0\`

- System.Buffers.dll

   `packages\System.Memory.4.5.3\lib\netstandard2.0\`

---

[1] Keep in mind that the SDK version number may be different in your case.

- System.Memory.dll

  packages\System.Runtime.CompilerServices.Unsafe.4.5.2\lib\
  netstandard2.0\

- System.Runtime.CompilerServices.Unsafe.dll

  packages\System.Reflection.Emit.Lightweight.4.6.0\lib\
  netstandard2.0\

- System.Reflection.Emit.Lightweight.dll

  C:\Program Files\Azure Kinect Body Tracking SDK\sdk\
  netstandard2.0\release\

- Microsoft.Azure.Kinect.BodyTracking.dll

- Microsoft.Azure.Kinect.BodyTracking.xml

Figure 3-2 shows the updated structure of your Unity project.

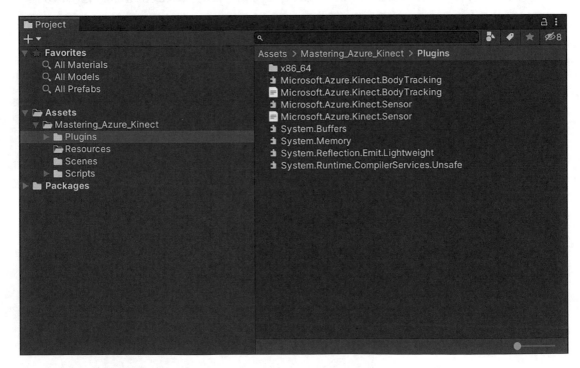

Figure 3-2. *The managed C# binary files*

Native C++ Binaries

Similar to the managed binaries, we are going to copy the native C++ ones. All of the following files should be copied under the `Plugins\x86_64` folder.

`packages\Microsoft.Azure.Kinect.Sensor.1.4.1\lib\native\amd64\release\`

- depthengine_2_0.dll

- k4a.dll

- k4arecord.dll

  `C:\Program Files\Azure Kinect Body Tracking SDK\tools\`

- k4abt.dll

- onnxruntime.dll

- onnxruntime_providers_shared.dll

- onnxruntime_providers_tensorrt.dll

- cudnn64_8.dll

- cudnn64_cnn_infer64_8.dll

- cudnn64_ops_infer64_8.dll

- cudart64_110.dll

- cublas64_11.dll

- cublasLt64_11.dll

- cufft64_10.dll

- directml.dll

- vcomp140.dll

- dnn_model_2_0_op11.onnx

- dnn_model_2_0_lite_op11.onnx

Your Unity Project view should look like Figure 3-3.

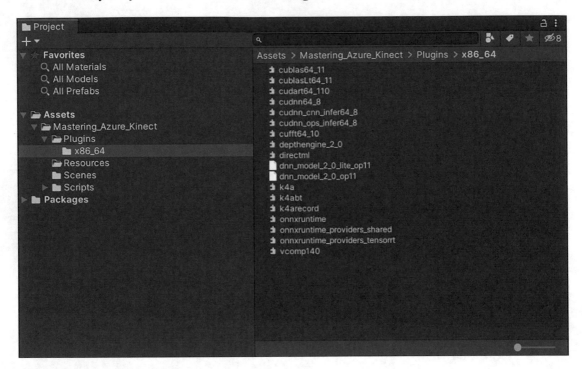

Figure 3-3. *The native C++ binary files (x86_64)*

The Machine Learning Models

Did you notice the extension of the last two dependency files? It's not ".dll", but ".onnx". As we mentioned in Chapter 2, body tracking is not a purely algorithmic process. Instead, it's relying on Artificial Intelligence. Machine Learning scientists are using smart containers that include sets of algorithms designed to recognize patterns. They process some input, feed it to multiple interconnected layers, and produce some output. Those smart containers are called **models,** and they encapsulate all of the body-tracking logic. In our case, the Machine Learning models are very special files named dnn_model_2_0_op11.onnx and dnn_model_2_0_lite_op11.onnx.[2]

---

[2] DNN stands for "Deep Neural Network," and it's a type of AI set of cognitive algorithms. ONNX stands for "Open Neural Network Exchange" and is an AI ecosystem. The ONNX Runtime is a low-level engine that processes the Machine Learning model to acquire its body-tracking results.

The structure of a Machine Learning model is, usually, pretty complex. I'm showing part of that structure in Figure 3-4. You don't need to dive deep into the art and science of Artificial Intelligence to understand body tracking, though. All you need to know is the following:

- The SDK is feeding the model with color and depth data.

- The model is processing the data, passing, and filtering them into multiple layers of algorithms. That is where the GPU is involved!

- Upon processing the data, the model outputs the 3D coordinates of the human body joints.

Why are there two model files? Wouldn't just one of them be enough? Microsoft initially released a single model file (`dnn_model_2_0_op11.onnx`). However, that model was too heavy for most computers. So the Microsoft team of AI scientists optimized the model and produced a new lighter one (`dnn_model_2_0_lite_op11.onnx`) that performs almost twice as fast by only compromising 5% of its tracking accuracy. It's also three times smaller in size. Even though it's preferred to go with the lighter model option, there may be use-case scenarios where high joint tracking precision is critical. On such occasions, you can programmatically opt for the heavy model to gain that extra 5% of accuracy.

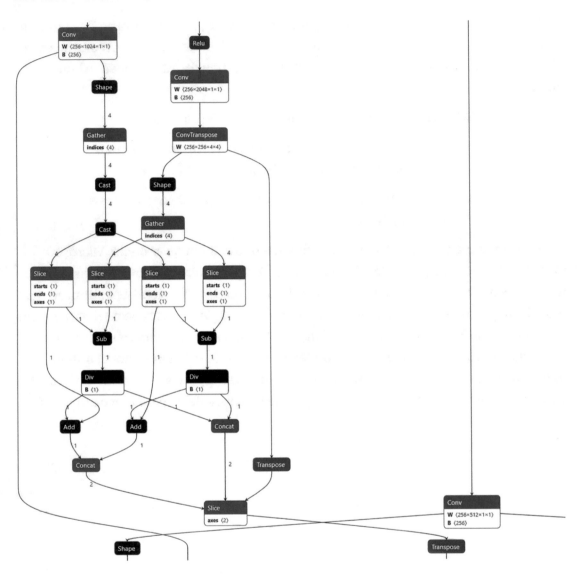

Figure 3-4. *Part of Microsoft's body-tracking model structure. The visualization was generated using Netron[3]*

---

[3] Netron model visualizer: https://lutzroeder.github.io/netron/

Running in the Editor

We've copied all dependencies to their proper locations, but there's one last step we need to make. Unity needs to locate some of the C++ binaries next to the project root folder. The project root is the parent of the Assets directory. Grab the following files and paste them there:

- onnxruntime.dll

- onnxruntime_providers_shared.dll

- onnxruntime_providers_tensorrt.dll

- cudnn64_8.dll

- cudnn64_cnn_infer64_8.dll

- cudnn64_ops_infer64_8.dll

- cudart64_110.dll

- cublas64_11.dll

- cublasLt64_11.dll

- cufft64_10.dll

- directml.dll

- vcomp140.dll

- dnn_model_2_0_op11.onnx

- dnn_model_2_0_lite_op11.onnx

So your root folder should look like Figure 3-5.

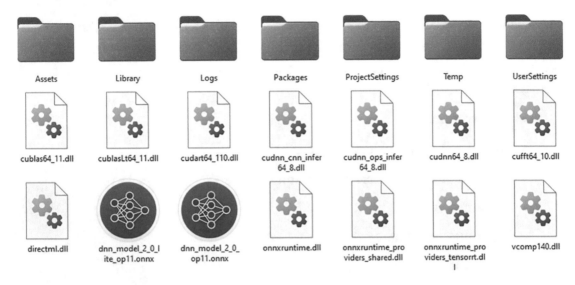

Figure 3-5. *The root Unity project folder*

If you've reached that far, the Unity Editor can now run Kinect applications using both the Sensor SDK and the Body Tracking SDK!

Deploying Your Unity Application

The Unity Editor is only a sandbox environment to test and debug your Unity applications. In a real-world scenario, you need to export your project as a Windows executable file. Go to **File ➤ Build Settings** and select to build for **PC, Mac & Linux Standalone**. Then, move to the right-hand options and specify the Target Platform and the Architecture of the executable:

- Target Platform: **Windows**

- Architecture: **x86_64**

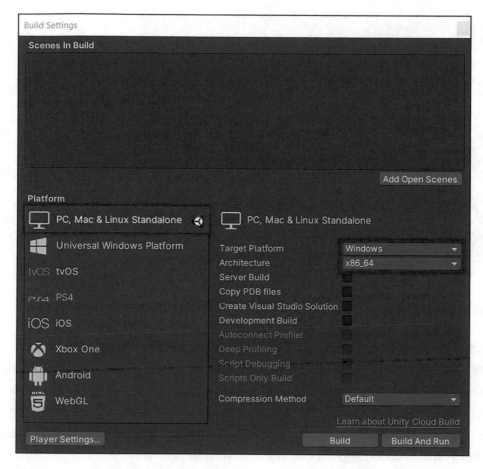

Figure 3-6. *The correct Unity build settings*

Attention!   Since we've only added Windows binaries (C++ DLLs), Unity3D will not be able to export the project on Linux. Supporting Linux is feasible, but it's outside the scope of this book. Moreover, be careful with the Architecture option: Kinect requires 64-bit processors, so the x86 option will not work because it's targeting 32-bit systems. You need to select the x86_64 option.

Do not forget to copy the .onnx and Body Tracking C++ .dll files next to your executable. **This is a critical step you should never miss!** If you don't copy the model and binary files next to your program, the application will not be able to use the Azure Kinect Body Tracking SDK properly. Your build folder should look similar to Figure 3-7.

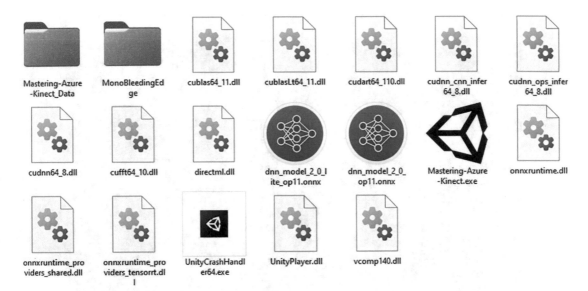

Figure 3-7. *The Unity build folder*

Congratulations! You have now created a bare-bones Kinect application using Unity3D. Of course, the application has no functionality, but it's working. I know this is not a straightforward way to build a project, as it involves a lot of "copy-paste hacking." However, as of the time of this writing, it's the only way to run Kinect applications and games in Unity3D. If you were building a traditional WinForms or WPF project, instead, you would only need to drop the C++ binaries next to your `.exe`.

Mastering Azure Kinect: Source Code

If the preceding process seems confusing, I've got you covered. Instead of copying and pasting the binary files every time you start a new project, you can download the Unity Package from the repository of this book.[4] Then, simply double-click the `.unitypackage` file, and Unity3D will launch automatically with all the required binaries loaded! The repository will be updated whenever a new version of the SDK is available by Microsoft. You can find the latest version under the "Releases"[5] section of the repository. Moreover, the complete source code examples of this book (plus any samples I may release in the future) will be freely available to you.

---

[4] Mastering Azure Kinect source code: `https://github.com/vangos/mastering-azure-kinect`

[5] Mastering Azure Kinect Unity package: `https://github.com/vangos/mastering-azure-kinect/releases/latest`

There is one other thing worth noting: The upcoming chapters are quite demanding, so I hate you having to deal with tedious issues, such as copying and pasting DLL files. I have created a C# script named `UnityEnvironment.cs`. That script runs automatically whenever you start or build your Unity project and checks whether the binaries are in place. If something is missing, the C# script will copy it to its proper location. Saying that, if you use the repository of this book, you have one less thing to worry about. Shift your focus to writing great Kinect code, instead.

Starting and Stopping the Device

Time to add some interactivity! Plug in your device and go back to the Unity Editor window. Create a new scene named **Azure_Kinect_Configuration**. Alternatively, open the corresponding scene from the repository of this book. Inside your scene, create an empty `GameObject` and attach a new script on it. Name the script `Azure_Kinect_Configuration.cs`. We'll use this script to start the device and experiment with various configurations.

The functionality of the Azure Kinect Sensor SDK is available in the `Microsoft.Azure.Kinect.Sensor` namespace. Open your C# script and import it:

```
using Microsoft.Azure.Kinect.Sensor;
```

Good! We now have access to the SDK classes and structures. We'll start by finding out the number of connected devices. Remember that we can connect more than one Kinect devices in a single computer. So checking the number of connected devices is an essential step since we need to ensure there is **at least one** device connected. We'll perform this check in our `Start()` method, which runs once the C# script is loaded.

```
private void Start()
{
    int deviceCount = Device.GetInstalledCount();

    Debug.Log($"Found {deviceCount} device(s).");
}
```

If you run this script with one sensor connected, the Console window should display the message **"Found 1 device(s)."**

Never miss this step in your code. Ever! Many things can go wrong if a user accidentally unplugs the cable or plugs it to a low-power USB port. Always ensure you are checking for connected devices before trying to access their streams.

Let's declare a new Kinect device object. The Kinect Device is the primary class we'll be using throughout all the subsequent examples to handle the physical hardware.

```
private Device _device;
```

We shall open the device only after we ensured it exists:

```
if (deviceCount > 0)
{
    _device = Device.Open();
}
```

The Open() method will open the default Kinect device. If you have more than one Kinect connected, you can specify the device index as follows:

```
if (deviceCount > 1) // Remember to check the range!
{
    _device = Device.Open(1); // Select the second device.
}
```

Device index starts at 0, which is the default device.

Save your script and run the program. The white light indicator of the Kinect device should open!

Of course, we need to close the device as well. When Kinect runs, lots of unmanaged resources are used. To release the unmanaged resources and gently close the device, you need to call the Dispose() method. If you don't do it, Unity will brutally kill the processes. Even worse, dangling pointers will remain after you stop the execution of the program! So implement the OnDestroy() Unity method, which is called when the script is unloaded, and close the Kinect device if it's not null.

```
private void OnDestroy()
{
    _device?.Dispose();
}
```

This is it! You have just written your very first Kinect program that properly opens and closes the device. Of course, there is much more you can do with the device.

Basic Device Properties

Every device has a set of unique hardware characteristics. The Device class allows you to access them all in one place. Hardware information includes the following:

- `SerialNum` – The unique serial number of the device

- `Version` – The hardware version number of cameras, microphones, and firmware

- `SyncInJackConnected`/`SyncOutJackConnected` – Indications whether other devices are connected to the synchronization pins

- `CurrentColorResolution` – The color resolution applied at any given moment

- `CurrentDepthMode` – The depth format and resolution applied at any given moment

For example, assume you want to know the serial number of your device. Simply access the `SerialNum` property:

```
Debug.Log($"Serial number: {kinect.SerialNum}");
```

Or let's say you have built the open source Sensor SDK from scratch and you need to know the firmware build type:

```
Debug.Log($"Firmware build type: {_device. kinect.Version.FirmwareBuild}");
```

Moving forward, we are going to apply different configuration settings and get some raw data.

Kinect Device Configuration

By default, the Kinect device has no configuration. Both color resolution and depth mode are set to **off**. Since Microsoft wants to provide the developers with as much customization as possible, this is a perfectly reasonable decision. The Azure Kinect Sensor SDK allows us to configure a lot of settings, the most important of which are the following:

- Frame rate – 5, 15, or 30 frames per second

- Color format – The encoding method of the video image (e.g., Motion JPEG, BGRA32)

- Color resolution – The resolution of the video image (e.g., 720p, 1080p, 3072p)

- Depth mode – The depth image format and resolution (e.g., WFOV or NFOV)

- Synchronized Images Only – Specifies whether the device will stream color and depth frames that arrived at the same time[6]

There are additional settings that handle multiple Kinect devices and enable or disable the light indicators. For now, we'll stick to the aforementioned five.

The settings are represented as simple Enumerations and Boolean properties. We are going to expose some common settings in the Editor, so we can switch values without having to edit the C# scripts directly. In order to display the settings in the Editor, create a new utility class and name it KinectConfiguration.cs and fill it with the information you would like to expose.

```
using System;
using Microsoft.Azure.Kinect.Sensor;
using UnityEngine;
```

---

[6] The video camera and the depth camera are different sensors; thus, they do not fire their frames at exactly the same time.

```
[Serializable]
public class KinectConfiguration
{
    [SerializeField] private FPS _cameraFps = FPS.FPS30;
    [SerializeField] private ImageFormat _colorFormat = ImageFormat.
    ColorBGRA32;
    [SerializeField] private ColorResolution _colorResolution =
    ColorResolution.R1080p;
    [SerializeField] private DepthMode _depthMode = DepthMode.NFOV_
    Unbinned;
    [SerializeField] private bool _synchronizedImagesOnly = true;

    public FPS CameraFps => _cameraFps;
    public ImageFormat ColorFormat => _colorFormat;
    public ColorResolution ColorResolution => _colorResolution;
    public DepthMode DepthMode => _depthMode;
    public bool SynchronizedImagesOnly => _synchronizedImagesOnly;
}
```

Then, in your initial Azure_Kinect_Configuration.cs file, reference the
KinectConfiguration class as an Editor field:

```
[SerializeField] private KinectConfiguration _configuration;
```

The preceding code will display the options in the form of check boxes and drop-downs, as seen in Figure 3-8. That's a great way to test different configurations quickly and speed up your development.

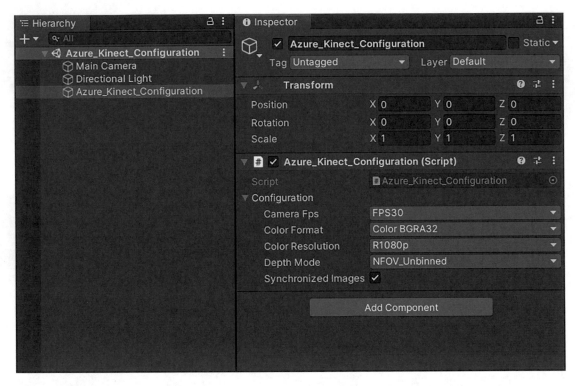

Figure 3-8. *The Azure Kinect configuration options, displayed in the Unity Inspector view*

So we can see the options, but how do we apply the desired settings on the `Device` object? Simple: We start the cameras and provide the configuration settings as a parameter of the `StartCameras()` method:

```
_device.StartCameras(new DeviceConfiguration
{
    CameraFPS = _configuration.CameraFps,
    ColorFormat = _configuration.ColorFormat,
    ColorResolution = _configuration.ColorResolution,
    DepthMode = _configuration.DepthMode,
    SynchronizedImagesOnly = _configuration.SynchronizedImagesOnly,
});
```

Pretty easy and straightforward, right? After you run the application, the light indicator of the Kinect should turn on. Feel free to play with the available options and run the program to ensure there are no surprises. After starting the camera, log the results to ensure you are getting the expected values:

```
Debug.Log($"Color Resolution: {_device.CurrentColorResolution}");

Debug.Log($"Depth Mode: {_device.CurrentDepthMode}");
```

> Opening the device and starting the cameras are different tasks. The Open() method is a prerequisite to use the cameras. The StartCameras() method is what begins video and depth streaming.

As you test the configurations in Unity, try to set the frame rate to "30" and the color resolution to "3072p." Click Run and see what happens.

Handling Invalid Configurations

If you followed my recommendation and requested a 4K resolution at 30 FPS, the application should have crashed by raising an exception. Why did that happen? Because such a configuration is invalid: The video camera cannot run at 30 FPS while streaming 4K video. Instead, you should have asked for 5 or 15 frames per second.

Saying that, you might wonder why Kinect does not automatically drop the frame rate or downscale the video. Kinect does not perform any type of automatic "fallback." It's your job as a responsible software developer to handle the exception and print a diagnostic message. Since the StartCameras() method is throwing the exception, we are going to wrap it in a try-catch block:

```
try
{
    _device.StartCameras(new DeviceConfiguration
    {
        CameraFPS = _configuration.CameraFps,
        ColorFormat = _configuration.ColorFormat,
        ColorResolution = _configuration.ColorResolution,
        DepthMode = _configuration.DepthMode,
```

```
        WiredSyncMode = _configuration.WiredSyncMode,
        SynchronizedImagesOnly = _configuration.SynchronizedImagesOnly,
        DisableStreamingIndicator = _configuration.
        DisableStreamingIndicator
    });
}
catch
{
    Debug.Log("Invalid camera configuration!");
}
```

Awesome! By this time, our application is gracefully handling different configuration scenarios, and our users are happy, as there will be no unexpected behaviors. Our Kinect device is ready to receive and process data.

Receiving Captures

Kinect will be streaming data for as long as it remains open. Streaming is not something that runs intermittently, though. Data is coming from the device in small time intervals, depending on the frame rate. For example, if you've selected to stream in 30 FPS, the application will receive one frame every 0.03 seconds, approximately. In Unity, we'll be checking for new frames in the Update() method. The SDK is grouping the raw data in a class called Capture. This is how you acquire a capture:

```
private void Update()
{
    using (Capture capture = _device.GetCapture())
    {
        // Do something with the capture.
    }
}
```

Notice we wrapped the capture in a `using` statement? That's because the capture needs to be disposed after we finish processing it. Disposable objects always include a `Dispose()` method that's releasing any unmanaged resources.[7] We can avoid calling the `Dispose()` method directly, while ensuring it will be invoked when necessary, by wrapping it into the `using` statement.

The `Capture` object encapsulates the information of the color and depth data, as well as general information about the frame. For example, we can display the temperature of the device:

```
using (Capture capture = _device.GetCapture())
{
    Debug.Log($"Temperature: {capture.Temperature}°C");
}
```

Experienced Unity developers may notice something weird: as we know, the `Update()` method is called whenever the screen refreshes its contents. Screens may refresh their contents 60, 90, or even 120 times per second. Consequently, the refresh rate of a screen is (usually) different to the refresh rate of Kinect and is affected by factors, such as the complexity of our application algorithms, the load of the CPU, or even by third-party processes. The frame rate is neither standard nor fixed. As a result, if the `Update()` method is called, let's say 90 times per second, and the device is streaming at 30 frames per second, you would be doing twice as many computations as you need, right? Well, not exactly.

The `GetCapture()` method does not simply return a reference to the latest capture. Instead, it's blocking the main thread until a new capture is available. It's only providing "fresh" data. But that's a problem too! What would happen if your application needs to perform operations that require a higher frame rate, such as animations or 3D rendering? Unity would hang! The `Update()` method would wait for the next frame blocking the user interface. If, for any reason, Kinect is not capable of streaming 30 frames per second, the application lag would not be acceptable.

---

[7] To create a disposable object yourself, simply implement the `IDisposable` C# interface.

There are many scenarios where you'd need to stream Kinect data from different threads. In that case, things get complicated. Rest assured as in the next chapters we are going to create our own background data provider. The background data provider will read the frames on a separate thread without blocking the main one. This way, our application's Update() method will only acquire the latest frame whenever necessary. No lag and no hangs!

There are two more checks you need to make. The first check is an easy guess: if there is no device connected to the computer, then the GetCapture() method would raise a NullReferenceException. At the beginning of the Update() method, check for null devices:

```
if (_device == null) return;
```

The second pitfall is a little harder to spot. Remember when we provided an invalid configuration to the device? In that case, the Device object would not be null, but its camera settings would be set to **off**. If you try to access the captured data, an Azure Kinect exception[8] would be raised. To avoid the exception, ensure the color resolution and the depth mode of the device are not set to off:

```
if (_device.CurrentColorResolution == ColorResolution.Off && _device.
CurrentDepthMode == DepthMode.Off) return;
```

Nobody wants an application that hangs unexpectedly or crashes miserably. That's the reason I'm insisting on best practices and adding security guards. If you've followed my advice up to this point, your app should be pretty much bulletproof.[9]

---

[8] The actual exception message would read "AzureKinectException: result = K4A_WAIT_RESULT_FAILED".

[9] There is no such thing as a fully bulletproof application. Things may go wrong, even if you think you've checked everything. For example, what happens if the user manually unplugs the Kinect cable while the app is in use? In that case, you should add a background process that's constantly checking for the number of connected devices. I'll leave this as an exercise for you.

Reading Data

The Azure Kinect SDK has gathered the data for us to use. The capture contains the properties of each stream type and everything we need to process them. Color and depth streams are expressed as a C# Image class. For example, we can retrieve the resolution of the color frame as follows:

```
using (Image color = capture.Color)
{
    Debug.Log($"Color: {color.WidthPixels}x{color.HeightPixels}");
}
```

Did you notice we, once again, wrapped the color image to a using statement? That's because the color image needs to release unmanaged resources once we are done with it.

Avoid disposing of the resources, and you will create a waterfall of memory leaks. If these objects remain undisposed, the computer memory will fill with unnecessary data, resulting in extensive hangs or, worse, out-of-memory crashes. Always use a using statement or call the Dispose() method directly.

In a similar way, we can acquire the width and height of the depth and infrared images. The complete source code of the Update() method, along with the control flow we've applied, is shown as follows:

```
private void Update()
{
    if (_device == null) return;
    if (_device.CurrentColorResolution == ColorResolution.Off && _device.
    CurrentDepthMode == DepthMode.Off) return;

    using (Capture capture = _device.GetCapture())
    {
        Debug.Log($"Temperature: {capture.Temperature}°C");

        using (Image color = capture.Color)
        using (Image depth = capture.Depth)
        using (Image ir = capture.IR)
```

```
        {
            Debug.Log($"Color: {color.WidthPixels}x{color.HeightPixels}");
            Debug.Log($"Depth: {depth.WidthPixels}x{depth.HeightPixels}");
            Debug.Log($"IR: {ir.WidthPixels}x{ir.HeightPixels}");
        }
    }
}
```

In the next two chapters, we are going to read the raw color and depth data, explore their properties further, and visualize the results.

When finished, remember to close the cameras before disposing of the Kinect device object:

```
private void OnDestroy()
{
    _device?.StopCameras();
    _device?.Dispose();
}
```

And there you have it: a functional Kinect application that's reading captures and displays information about the raw data. But most importantly, you have avoided lots of common pitfalls and gained complete control of your code.

Key Points

In this chapter, we started our coding journey using the Microsoft Azure Kinect SDK. Before moving forward, keep in mind the following:

- The SDK consists of native C++ and managed C# binaries. Download the binaries from NuGet and place them into the Unity Plugins folders. Along with the binaries, you should also copy the Machine Learning model file to the root of your project.

- Before accessing the Kinect device information, always check for the available connected devices.

- Open the Azure Kinect device and call the proper methods to start the cameras. When finished, stop the cameras and close the device to release its resources.

- Specify the desired configuration by assigning the configuration options when starting the cameras. Be careful to ensure the device supports your settings combination.

In the upcoming chapters, we'll start acquiring and displaying information from the Azure Kinect streams, beginning with the RGB color data.

CHAPTER 4

Color Data

Our world is a world of colors. As humans, we heavily rely on visual information to understand and process our environment. Our brain dedicates 140 million neurons to serve our visual cortex alone.[1] Even though a "sense hierarchy" may not exist, vision plays a crucial part in our daily lives, especially when it comes to our interaction with machines. It's no surprise the digital industry is tailored to please our eyes.

Microsoft has equipped Kinect with a first-class 4K video camera. So let's use that camera to acquire the color data and start building our Kinect visual interfaces.

Structure of a Color Frame

People see a picture or a video as a colorful image. Machines understand colors as sequences of bytes. For the computer's perspective, a video frame is simply a grid of red, green, and blue pixels. The video camera is streaming up to 30 still images per second – that's one image every 30 milliseconds. Since the images as served so quickly, our primitive brain perceives them as a moving clip. Each still image is called a "color frame" and has the following characteristics:

- Width and height

- Channels

- Data

If you draw a color image as a two-dimensional rectangle, the width and height are measured from the top-left corner, as shown in Figure 4-1.

---

[1] Leuba G; Kraftsik R (1994). "Changes in volume, surface estimate, three-dimensional shape and total number of neurons of the human primary visual cortex from midgestation until old age." Anatomy and Embryology.

© Vangos Pterneas 2022
V. Pterneas, *Mastering the Microsoft Kinect*, https://doi.org/10.1007/978-1-4842-8070-6_4

Figure 4-1. *A color frame served by the Azure Kinect SDK. The width and height are measured in terms of the top-left pixel*

Data refers to the actual colorful information of each pixel, while Channels refers to the number of color values we need to combine to draw a single pixel. The Azure Kinect SDK provides different methods of storing color information data. In this book, we'll explore two of them:

- The BGRA32 storage

- The MJPG storage

The BGRA storage method is the simplest form of storage, while the MJPG one is the fastest. If you master these two methods, I'm confident you can explore the rest of them independently. Figure 4-2 demonstrates the available color formats.

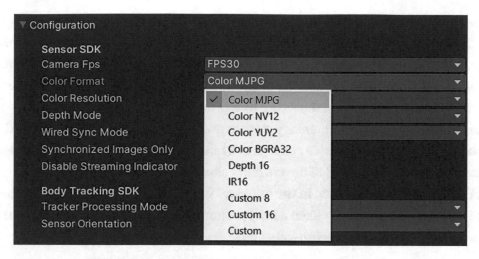

Figure 4-2. *The Azure Kinect color format options*

The BGRA32 Color Format

The BGRA32 format is the simplest way of storing color data. Every pixel is encoded as a set of four discrete color values:

- Blue

- Green

- Red

- Alpha transparency

The memory of a computer needs 8 bits (1 byte) to hold a single color value. As you know, the byte memory chunk is capable of storing numbers between 0 and 255. As a result, we can conveniently express the proportion of each color as a value between 0 and 255.

This way, computers can create millions of different colors by simply altering the proportions of blue, green, and red elements. Even a slight change in one element could result in a different combination, thus a different color.

The Alpha value specifies the transparency of the pixel. The lower the transparency value, the higher the opacity of the pixel, so you'll be able to see the background of the image more clearly. An Alpha value of 0 would result in full transparency, while an Alpha value of 255 would result in an opaque element. Since the Kinect video frames are not transparent, the Alpha value in the Azure Kinect SDK is always set to 255.[2]

Considering we need one memory byte for every channel, 4 bytes are required to store the whole pixel. Since 1 byte consists of 8 bits, the total number of bits necessary is 32, hence the name "BGRA32" of the current color format.

In Figure 4-3, I have zoomed in the original Kinect image, so I can show you the formation of the actual pixels. Given a high proportion of red and a low proportion of green and blue, we would get a brownish tint.

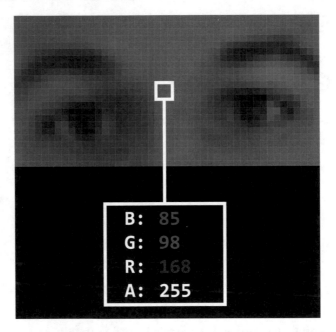

Figure 4-3.   *Each pixel is the result of four-color values: Blue, Green, and Red. In the Kinect SDK, the Alpha transparency is always set to 255*

Blue, Green, Red, and Alpha are the four channels of the BGRA32 color format. Storing the four-channel data into an array is quite tricky. Figure 4-4 showcases the correlation between the width, height, and channels of the color frame. Can you guess how many bytes would be necessary to store the BGRA information?

---

[2] Indeed, including a fixed Alpha value in every pixel results in very large arrays and decreased performance. That's why we'll explore more efficient methods later on.

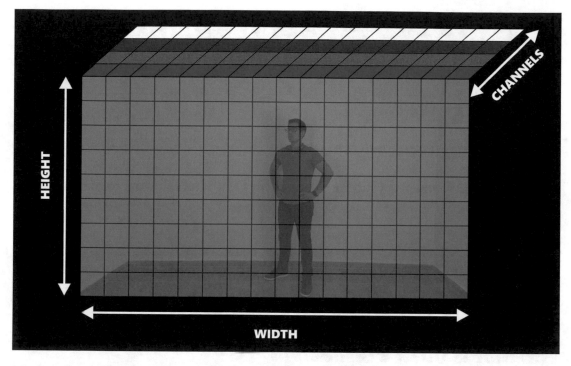

Figure 4-4. *A BGRA32 array with four channels (Blue, Green, Read, Alpha)*

At a high level, a video frame is a multidimensional array of size `width` × `height` × `channels`. However, computer RAM is linear storage, meaning it can only store one-dimensional data. As a result, Kinect needs to encode the raw bytes as a one-dimensional array. To do so, it's splitting the frame to rows and places each row after the other. The consecutive elements of the first row are followed by the successive elements of the second row, followed by the consecutive elements of the third row, etc. You may also hear of this method as "row-major order."

The length of each row is equal to the width of the frame times the channel (e.g., 1920×4). The number of rows is equal to the height of the frame (e.g., 1080). The total size of the 1D array would be `width` × `height` × `channels`. For example, 1920 × 1080 × 4 = 8,294,400 bytes.

Figure 4-5 shows the consecutive elements of a row. Keep in mind that we use four bytes for every pixel, and the bytes are stored sequentially.

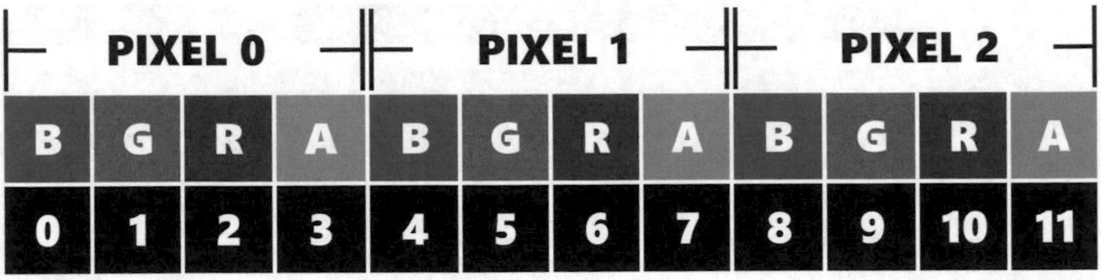

Figure 4-5. *One-dimensional array representation of a BGRA32 byte sequence*

The BGRA32 format is, by far, the simplest way to structure the raw color data and access them as a memory array. It's also easy to use and even easier to alter the data if you want to create visual effects.

However, when efficiency matters most, we need more performant ways to structure the data. Thankfully, the Kinect SDK provides an excellent compression method that allows us for optimum performance. Let's meet the MJPG color format.

The MJPG Color Format

The MJPG Kinect color format is an abbreviation for Motion JPEG[3] (or M-JPEG). Motion JPEG is a video compression format that relies on a simple principle. Instead of storing the color data as raw four-channel arrays, each video frame is compressed as a JPEG image. JPEG compression is a prevalent (and quite old) method of storing digital images.[4] The magic word here is "compression." Unlike the BGRA32 array we explored earlier, JPEG-encoded data are never in raw format. Instead, the image information has been reduced in a way that results in a much smaller size.

To begin with, the JPEG format provides no transparency; thus, the Alpha value of the raw data array is entirely removed. That results in 25% reduction in information! Of course, JPEG is way more than getting rid of unnecessary bytes. Here is how the JPEG compression algorithms work:[5]

---

[3] JPEG is also an acronym for "Joint Photographic Experts Group."

[4] Nowadays, computer scientists have come up with even better ways to store digital images, such as the WebP and HEIC formats. However, these formats are relatively new and there is no widespread adoption yet. On the other hand, the JPEG standard was formed in 1986 and has been officially around since 1992, so most computers, smartphones, and video cameras support it.

[5] In this book, we are examining the basic JPEG compression algorithm for reference purposes. If you want to learn more about the JPEG specification, visit https://jpeg.org.

- First, JPEG separates the luminance (a.k.a. intensity) and color components. The human eye is more sensitive to intensity than chrominance. As a result, we can compress color information without losing the details significantly. You can think of luminance as a grayscale representation of the original image. Shades of gray still preserve the visual intensity. The color information is further divided into blue-yellow components and red-green components.

- JPEG is downscaling the color components by some factor to reduce their size. We are referring to this process as "sub-sampling."

- After that, the image is divided into 8×8 blocks. JPEG performs mathematical transformations (Discrete Cosine Transform) to group the chroma information by the frequency of each color.

- Based on the desired level of compression, JPEG is then getting rid of some of the frequency information. The more data it discards, the lower the quality of the resulting image.

- Lastly, JPEG groups similar frequencies together, further reducing the size of the image.

As it becomes clear, the Motion-JPEG format comes at a trade-off: smaller size implies that less of the original image quality is preserved. That's why JPEG is called a "lossy" image compression method. However, for most use-case scenarios, Kinect included, the loss in quality is neglectable. As a result, it's worth the trade-off.

To read a JPEG-encoded image, we need to follow the aforementioned process in reverse order. Thankfully, Unity3D comes with a built-in JPEG decoder that does the heavy lifting right out of the box.

In the next section, we are going to see how to visualize the BGRA32 and the MJPG color stream formats in Unity3D.

Displaying Color Data in Unity3D

Up to this point, you have a deep understanding of the underlying color encoding mechanisms. It's time to visualize the information in Unity3D. To display the color information, we are going to create a new scene with two elements:

- One `RawImage` component

- One empty `GameObject` component with its corresponding C# script

In my project, I have named the scene Azure_Kinect_Color, and it looks like Figure 4-6.

Figure 4-6. *A Unity scene with a Raw Image UI component*

Specifying the Color Configuration

In your empty GameObject component, add a script referencing the Kinect configuration and the Raw Image:

```
[SerializeField] private KinectConfiguration _configuration;
[SerializeField] private RawImage _image;
```

Do not forget to assign the UI component you created in the Editor to the RawImage component you declared in the C# file.[6] Additionally, declare the Kinect device to use, as well as a 2D texture to store the color information:

```
private Device _kinect;
private Texture2D _texture;
```

---

[6] Alternatively, simply download the source code of the book and find all the information ready for use.

Just like we did in Chapter 3, start the Kinect cameras in your Start() method.

For clarity reasons, the following code omits the checks for connected devices or null device objects. As we discussed in Chapter 3, you should always perform these checks in real-world applications.

```
private void Start()
{
    _kinect = Device.Open();

    _kinect.StartCameras(new DeviceConfiguration
    {
        // Fill-in as in Chapter 3.
    });

    int colorWidth = _kinect.GetCalibration().
            ColorCameraCalibration.ResolutionWidth;
    int colorHeight = _kinect.GetCalibration().
            ColorCameraCalibration.ResolutionHeight;
}
```

Do not forget to close the cameras and dispose of the Kinect sensor when the program finishes running:

```
private void OnDestroy()
{
    _kinect?.StopCameras();
    _kinect?.Dispose();
}
```

Up to this point, the C# code should be familiar to you. Whenever you change the color format in the Inspector window, Kinect will serve a different byte array. Now, it's time to add some spice.

Reading Kinect Color Data as BGRA32

BGRA32-encoded byte arrays have a fixed size equal to width × height × channels. The 2D texture we declared previously will hold the raw BGRA data. Let's initialize the texture with the proper width, height, and format information. Append the following code into your Start() method:

```
_texture = new Texture2D
(
    colorWidth,
    colorHeight,
    TextureFormat.BGRA32,
    false
);

_image.texture = texture;
```

We constructed a texture and assigned it to the Raw Image component we created in the Editor.

In the Update() method, we are going to grab the color frames, acquire their data, and feed them to the texture. The color data are stored in memory as low-level arrays. To interact with low-level data, we need to use the MemoryMarshal class. MemoryMarshal is a handy intermediate utility for handling unmanaged data. It's part of the System. Runtime.InteropServices namespace, found in the System.memory.dll. As you can see in the following code snippet, C# provides a self-explanatory syntax to convert the low-level data into a traditional C# byte array.

```
private void Update()
{
    using (Capture capture = _kinect.GetCapture())
    using (Image color = capture.Color)
    {
        byte[] colorData =
            MemoryMarshal.AsBytes(color.Memory.Span)
            .ToArray();

        _texture.LoadRawTextureData(colorData);
        _texture.Apply();
    }
}
```

To update the texture, all we need to do is call the `LoadRawTextureData()` and `Apply()` methods. If you click the Play button, you should finally see the live camera feed!

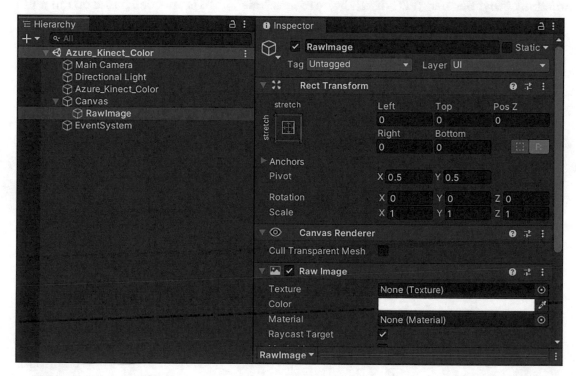

Figure 4-7. *The live Kinect video camera feed*

Reading Kinect Color Data as MJPG

The process of reading MJPG-encoded data is quite similar to BGRA32. Keep in mind that MJPG-encoded arrays do not have a fixed size because JPEG compression results in different binary data depending on the original color information. Moreover, the JPEG information is in RGB format, which is three-channel information. Thus, we should initialize the texture with the RGB24 format.

```
_texture = new Texture2D
(
      colorWidth,
      colorHeight,
TextureFormat.RGB24,
      false
);
```

The Kinect API is consistent, so we'll use the MemoryMarshal class to read the color data once again. Be careful, though! This time, we should not call the LoadRawTextureData() method. Why? Because JPEG data is by no means "raw"! JPEG is encoded based on the JPEG specification. Instead, Unity provides the LoadImage() method, which properly decodes the JPEG information and updates the texture accordingly.

```
private void Update()
{
    using (Capture capture = _kinect.GetCapture())
    using (Image color = capture.Color)
    {
        byte[] colorData =
                MemoryMarshal.AsBytes(color.Memory.Span)
                .ToArray();

        _texture.LoadImage(colorData);
    }
}
```

The result of running the project should be identical to Figure 4-7 – only faster. To understand precisely how faster MJPG is compared to BGRA32, feel free to measure the execution time of each method. That would be a great exercise that will show you why every millisecond matters.

Key Points

In this chapter, we explored the Azure Kinect video camera data. You've learned about the different streaming data formats and investigated the differences between the raw BGRA32 format and the MJPG one. We also displayed the color data using the built-in Unity methods. Moving forward, keep in mind the following:

- Kinect serves color frames of different size (width and height).

- Each frame has a specific number of channels based on its format.

- BGRA32 is a raw data format with four channels.

- MJPG is a compressed data format with three channels.

- MJPG is faster than BGRA32.

- The Kinect SDK allows us to access the color data using the same API

- To convert the native data into a C# byte array, we are using the handy `MemoryMarshal` class.

In the upcoming chapter, we are going to apply similar techniques to acquire and visualize the depth data.

CHAPTER 5

Depth Data

The ability to see the world in 3D is what makes Kinect unique. We have already explored how the depth camera works in Chapter 1. Like the process we followed with the color video camera, we'll now focus on acquiring data from the depth sensor.

Structure of a Depth Frame

Just a quick reminder of how the depth sensor works: first, it's emitting an infrared light pulse. Then, the physical points reflect the pulse back to the sensor. Upon receiving the pulse, the sensor measures the time it took it to return. If the pulse took too long, it means the object is far from the sensor. On the other hand, if the pulse returned quickly, the object is close to the device.[1]

Repeat the preceding process for thousands of light rays simultaneously, and you'll get the distance of thousands of points. How many points? Well, for a resolution of 512×512, that's 262,144 measurements! Just like color frames, depth frames also have width and height properties, specifying how many points the field of view can "see" horizontally and vertically. This time, each point is not a blend of red, blue, and green colors but rather a single distance measurement.

Internally, the depth processor is organizing all these distance measurements, producing a *depth map* structure. A depth map is nothing but a collection of distance values at their respective positions, as illustrated in Figure 5-1.

---

[1] If you are familiar with the old Kinect or other depth sensors, you know there are some edge cases here. For example, some materials may absorb the infrared light, while others may reflect it to a different location. As a result, the pulse may never return back to the emitter. We'll see how to handle such cases at the end of this chapter.

© Vangos Pterneas 2022
V. Pterneas, *Mastering the Microsoft Kinect*, https://doi.org/10.1007/978-1-4842-8070-6_5

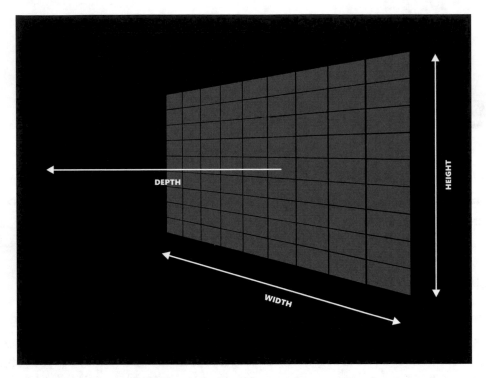

Figure 5-1. *Representation of a Kinect depth frame. Each pixel has its unique position in the horizontal and vertical axis and its depth value measurement*

Every depth map element has an X dimension (horizontal), a Y dimension (vertical), and a Z dimension (depth). The horizontal and vertical dimensions specify the position of the point within the frame, thus measured in pixels. The depth values are measured in **millimeters**. For example, a physical point may be located at pixel [128, 52] and have a depth value of 2710. Remember that we start counting from the top-left pixel.

Internally, the raw data of a depth frame is stored as a one-dimensional array, as shown in Figure 5-2.

PIXEL 0	PIXEL 1	PIXEL 2	PIXEL 3
5128	4950	5088	4942

Figure 5-2. *Raw depth data representation as a 1D array of unsigned short values*

There is a good reason why depth measurements are stored in millimeters: first, a millimeter is a submultiple of meter, the official unit of the Metric system.[2] Second, computers can store millimeters as integer values. Let's assume that an object is positioned 1.25 meters from the camera, which is precisely 1250 millimeters. If we needed to store the value in meters, we would need a floating-point number (in C#, a float requires 4 bytes of memory). Alternatively, storing millimeters would need an unsigned short integer number, which occupies half-space (2 bytes of memory). Keep in mind that we are talking about hundreds of thousands of points, right? It's impressive how a simple technique like this can save us 50% of memory usage.

As you can see, the depth frame is, once again, a one-dimensional array of raw data values. At first, that seems confusing. Remember: The array data structure is simply a means of storing and representing the physical values. In the color frame, we describe each color as a triad of red, blue, and green values. Similarly, the depth frame represents each point as a numeric distance value.

Obviously, depth values cannot be negative. Kinect is measuring every distance relative to itself and can only see objects in front of it. As a result, negative depth values would mean that an item is behind the camera.

Narrow and Wide Fields of View

The Azure Kinect depth sensor supports two ways to view the physical space, or two different fields of view: narrow field of view (NFOV) and wide field of view (WFOV). What's the difference? The NFOV can see a smaller portion of the physical world within a longer distance. Its viewing angle is 75°×65°. On the other hand, the WFOV can capture a much larger extent of the world within a shorter operating range. Its wide viewing angle is almost double the narrow one, at 120°×120°.

---

[2] If you are using the US/Imperial measurement system, please refer to the Appendix chapters of the book.

Figures 5-3 and 5-4 display the same scene captured using the NFOV and WFOV modes, respectively. You can immediately notice the trade-off: more details in the first image, but more space in the second one. The dark areas on the floor and ceiling indicate that the pixels were invalidated due to, for example, reflections. Sometimes, as you are watching a continuous stream of depth frames, you may notice "flying pixels" in the depth images; these are nothing but dust particles momentarily reflecting the IR beans.

Figure 5-3. *The narrow field of view (NFOV)*

Figure 5-4. *The equivalent wide field of view (WFOV)*

Once again, it becomes apparent that we need to compromise something (e.g., the field of view) to gain something else (e.g., range). As a software engineer, you should carefully examine your use-case scenario and select the depth operation mode that fits best. For example, if you need to track a vast scene where objects only matter within a few feet, go for the WFOV option. If you need to measure objects in longer distances more precisely, the NFOV would be the way to go. Body-tracking applications analyzing the human range of motion would benefit from using the NFOV.

Kinect also incorporates an additional trick to extend the depth range on both the NFOV and WFOV. The technique is called **analog binning** and is increasing the depth range by up to 30%. For example, the NFOV unbinned option can reliably see objects placed between 0.5 and 3.86 meters. However, if you select the NFOV binned option, the operating range increases to 5.46 meters! Of course, there is a catch: the unbinned option will give you a resolution of 640×576, while the binned option will only provide 320×288 points.

As a result, you need to select not only between narrow and wide FOV but also between the binned and the unbinned options! Sounds confusing? Table 5-1 is illustrating what to expect from every possible configuration combination.[3]

Table 5-1. *All of the Azure Kinect Depth mode combinations*

FOV	Angle	Binning	Resolution	Range (meters)
NFOV	75°×65°	Unbinned	640×576	0.5–3.86
NFOV	75°×65°	Binned	320×288	0.5–5.46
WFOV	120°×120°	Unbinned	1024×1024[4]	0.25–2.21
WFOV	120°×120°	Binned	512×512	0.25–2.88

Back to Unity3D, the DepthMode enumeration we exposed in the Editor allows you to quickly switch between the preceding modes or even turn off the depth sensor entirely.

---

[3] Investigating the internal mechanisms of the depth camera is outside the scope of this book. However, if you are curious to learn more about the analog binning in Time-of-Flight technology, refer to Microsoft's whitepaper here: https://docs.microsoft.com/en-us/windows/mixed-reality/out-of-scope/isscc-2018

[4] Again, high resolution comes at a cost: when using WFOV at 1024×1024 (1MP), the frame rate is limited to 15 FPS. In contrast, all the other combinations support running at 30 FPS.

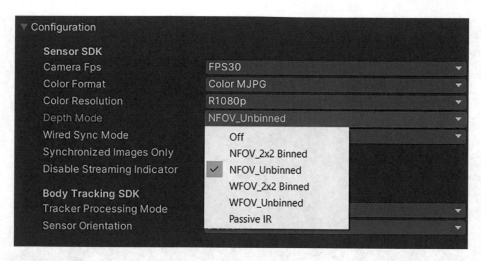

Figure 5-5. *The Azure Kinect depth mode options*

The **Passive IR** mode is a special type of depth mode that only observes the environment lighting (also known as *ambient illumination*). Unlike the other modes, this one does not provide depth/distance information. Instead, it's only measuring how much light the physical objects are emitting.

Now that we have a good understanding of the ins and outs of the depth camera, let's capture and visualize depth frames in Unity3D.

Displaying Depth Data in Unity3D

Now that you know what depth frames consist of, you may wonder how we will visualize a map of distances on a two-dimensional screen. After all, our eyes cannot "see" lengths, only colors. You may have noticed those grayscale or rainbow depth pictures already. Let's see how to create colors from meters.

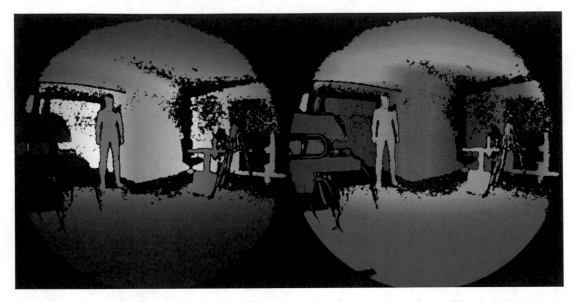

Figure 5-6. *Grayscale depth visualization (left) vs. rainbow depth visualization (right)*

Even though it may seem counterintuitive, visualization of depth data relies on an elementary principle: *we map a range of distances to a range of colors.*

If you refer to Table 5-1, you already know the operating depth range. So let's say you select the NFOV unbinned setting. The minimum depth distance would be 0.5 meters (closest), while the maximum distance would be 5.46 meters (farthest). In a grayscale visualization, you have shades of gray, ranging from black (0) to white (255). If black corresponds to the minimum distance and white corresponds to the maximum distance, we can colorize every intermediate-depth value as a different shade of gray!

If grayscale is too dull, I will also show you how to create a rainbow-like effect, also known as *jet color map.* The jet color map relies on the same principle. Close distances are displayed as shades of blue, intermediate distances as shades of green-yellow, and long distances as shades of orange-red.

Without further ado, launch Unity3D and create a new scene. Just like we did in the color visualization scene in Chapter 4, we are also going to create two elements:

- One RawImage component to display the depth data

- One empty GameObject to assign the configuration options and write the C# logic

As you can see in Figure 5-7, I have also exposed an enumeration value indicating the depth visualization color map – grayscale or jet.

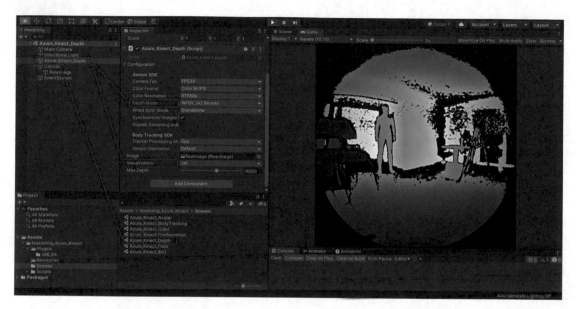

Figure 5-7. *A Unity scene with Editor options for depth visualization*

Depth Configuration and Data

The setup of the new scene is identical to the color scene. In your empty GameObject, add the necessary references to the Kinect configuration and the RawImage component:

```
[SerializeField] private KinectConfiguration _configuration;
[SerializeField] private RawImage _image;
```

Don't forget to drag and drop the RawImage component to the C# script. Then, declare the Kinect device reference, as well as the texture reference:

```
private Device _kinect;
private Texture2D _texture;
```

Last but not least, create a simple enumeration that allows you to change the depth visualization at runtime:

```
enum DepthVisualization
{
    Gray,
    Jet
}
```

```
[SerializeField] private DepthVisualization _visualization;
```

Back to the trivial, yet essential, staff, open and close the camera as necessary. This time, we'll acquire the depth resolution from the device calibration class and initialize the texture accordingly:

```
private void Start()
{
    _kinect = Device.Open();

    _kinect.StartCameras(new DeviceConfiguration
    {
        // Fill-in as in Chapter 3.
    });

    int depthWidth = _kinect.GetCalibration().
        DepthCameraCalibration.ResolutionWidth;
    int depthHeight = _kinect.GetCalibration().
        DepthCameraCalibration.ResolutionHeight;

    _texture = new Texture2D
        (
            depthWidth,
            depthHeight,
            TextureFormat.RGB24,
            false
        );

    _image.texture = _texture;
}
```

```
private void OnDestroy()
{
    _kinect?.StopCameras();
    _kinect?.Dispose();
}
```

Did you notice that we created an RGB-formatted texture? Depth data are distances, but screen colors are still pairs of good old red, green, and blue values.

Moving forward, we can capture the depth data in Unity's Update() method. We'll be, once again, using the MemoryMarshal class to access the low-level array. Using MemoryMarshal, we'll convert the raw binary data to unsigned short (ushort) integer values. The ushort structure holds positive integers between 0 and 65,535.

```
private void Update()
{
    using (Capture capture = _kinect.GetCapture())
    using (Image depth = capture.Depth)
    {
        ushort[] depthData =
            MemoryMarshal.Cast<byte, ushort>
            (depth.Memory.Span).ToArray();

        byte[] pixels =
            _visualization == DepthVisualization.Gray
            ? Gray(depthData)
            : Jet(depthData);

        _texture.LoadRawTextureData(pixels);
        _texture.Apply();
    }
}
```

Then, depending on the colorization selection, we'll visualize the depth data in grayscale or jet form. It's apparent that we need to create a new byte array of the depth data and feed it to our texture. The implementation of the Gray() and Jet() methods is discussed in the following.

Grayscale Depth Visualization

The grayscale map is the most straightforward depth visualization. Each distance value is mapped between 0 and 255. To do so, we need to loop within the depth list. Upon acquiring the current depth value, we apply the rule of three to find the direct proportion within the 0–255 range. Keep in mind that our method returns a colorized image, so it needs to be an RGB-encoded array of byte data.

```
private byte[] Gray(ushort[] data)
{
    const int channels = 3;              // RGB
    const byte maxByte = byte.MaxValue;  // 255
    const ushort maxDepth = 5460;        // 5.46 meters

    byte[] pixels = new byte[data.Length * channels];

    for (int i = 0; i < data.Length; i++)
    {
        ushort depth = data[i];

        if (depth > 0)
        {
            byte gray =
                    (byte)((float)depth / maxDepth * maxByte);

            pixels[i * channels + 0] = gray;
            pixels[i * channels + 1] = gray;
            pixels[i * channels + 2] = gray;
        }
    }

    return pixels;
}
```

Jet Depth Visualization

The jet color map is a little more complex to implement. In this case, we need to map each distance value between -1 and +1 and, then, proportionally create the red, green, and blue pixels.

```csharp
private byte[] Jet(ushort[] data)
{
    const int channels = 3;              // RGB
    const byte maxByte = byte.MaxValue; // 255
    const ushort maxDepth = 5460;        // 5.46 meters

    byte[] pixels = new byte[data.Length * channels];

    float min = -1.0f;
    float max = 1.0f;

    for (int i = 0; i < data.Length; i++)
    {
        ushort depth = data[i];

        if (depth > 0)
        {
            float t =
                    depth * (max - min) / maxDepth + min;

            float red = Mathf.Clamp01
                (1.5f - Mathf.Abs(2.0f * t - max)) * maxByte;

            float green = Mathf.Clamp01
                (1.5f - Mathf.Abs(2.0f * t)) *
                maxByte;

            float blue = Mathf.Clamp01
                (1.5f - Mathf.Abs(2.0f * t + max)) * maxByte;

            pixels[i * channels + 0] = (byte)red;
            pixels[i * channels + 1] = (byte)green;
            pixels[i * channels + 2] = (byte)blue;
        }
    }

    return pixels;
}
```

Ambiguous Depth Cases

Depth cameras are not perfect. It's impossible to capture a 3D scene without a margin of error. The images I've demonstrated during the whole chapter include black spaces that mysteriously exist in various places within the scene. These black pixels indicate that their depth values are open to more than one interpretation. Actually, there are five primary causes of ambiguity:

1. Too close to the camera

2. Too far from the camera

3. Object edges

4. Moving objects

5. Corners

The depth sensor considers all of these cases as invalid, thus assigning them a distance of **zero**. Notice the black "gaps" in the images of the following sections.

Too Close to the Camera or Too Far from the Camera

This scenario is fairly apparent. Since the depth camera has a specific range, anything that's outside that range will be invisible. The book is over-exposed and saturates the pixels.

Figure 5-8. *A book that is positioned 0.15 meters in front of the camera. Kinect cannot see it because the book needs to be at least 0.25 meters far*

Object Edges

The edges of objects receive an infrared signal from both the background and foreground. Mixed infrared signals result in what is displayed as a black contour around the object.

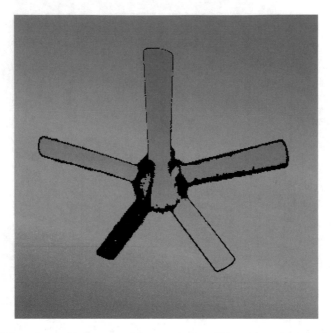

Figure 5-9. *Visible edges of a static object. Hint: The item is a ceiling fan*[5]

Moving Objects

When an object is in fast motion, the preceding effect becomes way more obvious. The signal from background and foreground points is almost entirely invalidating itself.

---

[5] I know, it looks like an Andy Warhol painting.

Figure 5-10. *The same ceiling fan, only this time it's moving*

Corners

Have you ever tried to point Kinect to a conjunction of two walls? Even though the corner is perfectly still and remains within the valid depth range, it still appears black. The reason is the infrared beam from the sensor is reflected off one wall and onto the other. This reflection comes back both directly and via the walls, so it is causing ambiguity; thus, the pixels are invalidated. The phenomenon is called multipath and is very common in most commercial depth cameras.

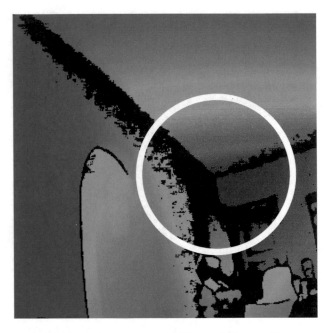

Figure 5-11. *A corner formed from two walls and the ceiling*

Key Points

In this chapter, we explored the Azure Kinect depth data. You've learned about the supported fields of view and their respective operating range. We also explored how to apply different effects to convert the depth information into colorful visualizations. Here are the key takeaways of this chapter:

- The Azure Kinect depth camera supports two different fields of view: narrow and wide.

- Kinect applies optional analog binning to increase the range of the camera.

- Different binning modes result in different depth frame resolutions.

- A depth frame is an array of distance values.

- To visualize the depth frames, we map the distance values to a specified color range.

- Typical depth visualizations include grayscale (black to white) and jet (blue to green to red).

- There are cases of ambiguous depth measurements, such as object edges, corners, and fast-moving objects.

Moving forward, we will see how the Azure Kinect SDK is combining color and depth data to track human body joints!

CHAPTER 6

Body Tracking

Depth cameras have many practical, real-world applications, from 3D object scanning to environment understanding, to Augmented Reality. Since 2009, though, Kinect has been famous for one thing: human body tracking.

Human body tracking revolutionized the way people interacted with computers and opened a world of possibilities. Body tracking is the ability to detect skeleton joints using depth or color image data. The Kinect technology can identify the coordinates of the points that belong to a specific person and output their positions in 3D. Why is this information so important? In health care and fitness, developers can measure the range of motion and provide smart rehabilitation. In manufacturing, Kinect systems can analyze worker behavior, performance, and safety. When used in Robotics, autonomous systems can map their surroundings and imitate human movement.

The original Kinect for XBOX 360 had an exceptionally memorable pitch to describe its functionality: "you are the controller." Microsoft envisioned a future beyond keyboards and mice. It was a future of natural interaction with computers. Even though that vision came true via the HoloLens device, Kinect set the path to natural user interaction due to its remarkable skeleton tracking functionality.

The Technology of Body Tracking

Back in 2009, computer performance was only a fraction of what it is today,[1] and Artificial Intelligence was not a household name yet. When people were talking about AI, they mostly referred to science fiction movies. But Microsoft Research was planning a giant leap forward that would dramatically change our perception of what's possible.

---

[1] I'm writing these lines in 2020 AD.

V. Pterneas, *Mastering the Microsoft Kinect*, https://doi.org/10.1007/978-1-4842-8070-6_6

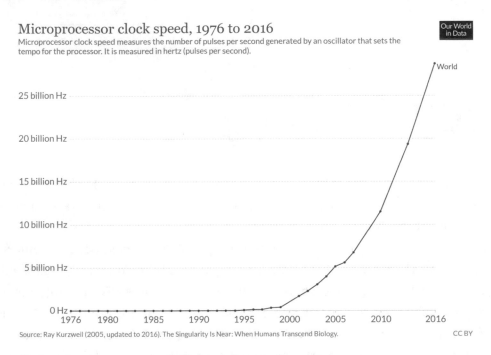

Microprocessor clock speed, 1976 to 2016

Figure 6-1. Microprocessor clock speed over the years

Considering the limited capabilities of a typical home computer or XBOX console, Microsoft needed to develop a body-tracking system that could run efficiently and reliably in real time. Their solution was based on a classic yet brilliantly applied pattern recognition algorithm.[2] First, Microsoft Research trained a classifier using a varied annotated dataset. Then, the algorithm was assigned a probability score on the pixels of a depth image. Simply put, a depth pixel could be part of an arm or leg, with different probability scores. Combining the probabilities of every pixel, Microsoft was then able to reconstruct the skeleton model and detect the human joints' relative positions.

---

[2] You can read the complete algorithm and scientific paper here: `www.microsoft.com/en-us/ research/publication/real-time-human-pose-recognition-in-parts-from-a-single- depth-image`

 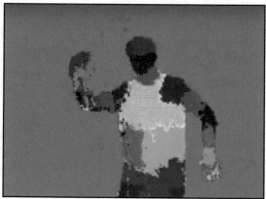

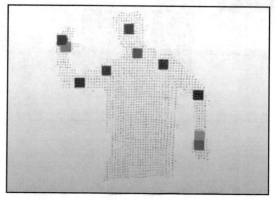

Figure 6-2. *Simplified human joint detection algorithm. From depth data to body part estimations to joint coordinates. Image adapted by Microsoft Research*

The New Azure Kinect Approach

The algorithm described was used by the initial Kinect for XBOX 360 and the subsequent Kinect for Windows SDKs. Nowadays, processing power has skyrocketed, and Machine Learning scientists are utilizing the graphics processing unit for complex calculations. So the new Azure Kinect takes the original body-tracking approach many steps further.

The software is more heavily relying on Machine Learning and starts with a 2D approach. First, the Azure Kinect SDK is acquiring the depth and infrared images. Then, it feeds the infrared image to a neural network and extracts the 2D joint coordinates and the silhouette of the users. Each 2D pixel is assigned the corresponding depth value from the depth frame, thus giving its position in the 3D space. The results are postprocessed to produce accurate human body skeletons.[3]

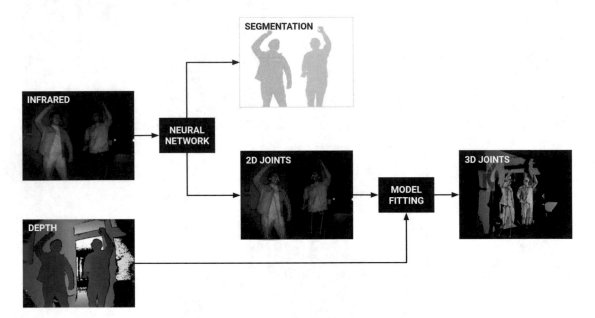

Figure 6-3. *Infrared and depth data combined to extract the 2D and 3D joint coordinates. Image adapted by Microsoft Research*

The new approach comes with significant benefits compared to its counterparts:

- Higher joint tracking accuracy and precision

- Support for challenging poses (standing, sitting, lying, bending)

- Additional body landmarks (e.g., eyes, ears, nose, clavicles)

- No limit to the number of tracked people[4]

---

[3] The slides of the official Microsoft presentation are available here: www.microsoft.com/en-us/research/project/skeletal-tracking-on-azure-kinect/

[4] The old Kinect devices could track up to six people. Azure Kinect has no built-in limit, but you should avoid using it in overcrowded environments. When used with more than ten people, Kinect could easily mismatch their joints.

Considering all these improvements, the new Azure Kinect can be now used reliably in demanding applications, such as health care or automation. On the downside, all this AI processing requires a high-end GPU. Microsoft recommends an NVIDIA GTX 1070 or better; however, individual tests show that even a GTX 1050 would be capable of running body-tracking applications.

Structure of a Human Body

We know that Kinect can track human bodies. In programming terms, what exactly is a body? Every human body, along with its joints' properties, is represented as a high-level C# class. Thankfully for developers, the Azure Kinect Body Tracking SDK is doing all of the heavy lifting for us.

Each body instance has a **unique identifier** (ID) and a **collection of joints**. The ID of the body is simply a numeric value that distinguishes one body from another. That's particularly useful when there are many people within the field of view, and you need to track a specific one. The joint collection holds a list of Joint structures with their corresponding properties. Let's explore the members of the joint structure further.

Joint ID

Kinect tracks two types of points: skeletal joints and facial landmarks. Skeletal joints are actual connections between human bones, such as the shoulders, elbows, wrists, knees, and feet. Facial landmarks include parts of the face and, more specifically, the eyes, ears, and nose. From now on, and for the sake of convenience, we'll be referring to both joints and landmarks simply as "joints." The ID is the unique name or type of each joint. In C#, the IDs of the joints are exposed in the JointId enumeration. Kinect tracks the following joints per person:

- Pelvis

- Spine naval

- Spine chest

- Neck

- Left/right clavicle

- Left/right shoulder

- Left/right elbow

- Left/right wrist

- Left/right hand

- Left/right handtip

- Left/right thumb

- Left/right hip

- Left/right knee

- Left/right ankle

- Left/right foot

- Head

- Nose

- Left/right eye

- Left/right ear

Figure 6-4 displays the preceding joints on top of a humanoid figure, so you know precisely where each joint is supposed to be.

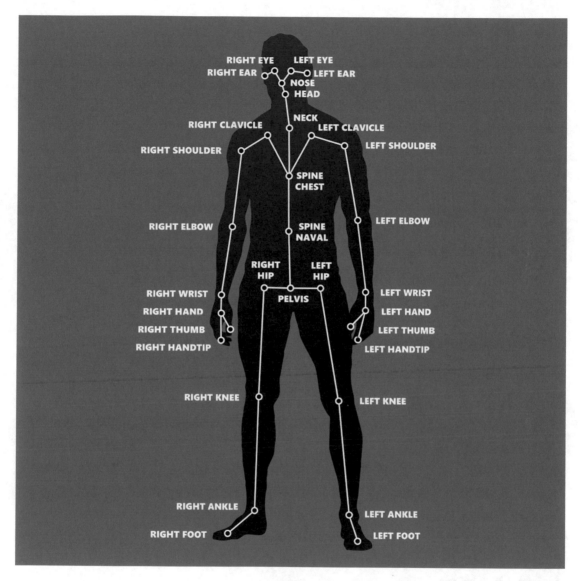

Figure 6-4. *The Azure Kinect–supported human body joints*

As you can see, Kinect recognizes 32 joints! Want to track the left shoulder? Simply call the proper member of the JointId enumeration (e.g., JointId.ShoulderLeft). The JointId enumeration also includes a member named Count. That is not an actual joint; instead, it's used to access the number of joints easily.

Joint Confidence Level

People may stand in front of the camera in a lot of different ways. There are inconvenient cases where not every single joint is visible. Some joints may be outside the field of view or even behind physical objects. Other joints may move too quickly. In either case, developers need to know whether a joint is tracked reliably before using it. That's why the Joint structure includes a property named ConfidenceLevel. The ConfidenceLevel allows us to know just how well Kinect is monitoring each joint. There are four levels of confidence:

- **High** – Kinect is tracking this joint reliably.

- **Medium** – Kinect is tracking the joint with average confidence.

- **Low** – The joint is probably occluded, so Kinect is predicting its position. A joint with low confidence is not visible. Instead, the SDK is internally trying to estimate its coordinates based on neighboring joints.

- **None** – The joint is totally off the field of view.

As a software developer, you need to take the confidence levels seriously. Imagine you are working on a health-care application, and you are trying to measure the range of motion of the spine. If the spine joints have a confidence level of Low or None, the measurements will be irrelevant. Before accessing vital information, always check the confidence level of the joints that matter!

Joint Position

The Azure Kinect SDK is providing the coordinates of joints in the 3D space. What are those coordinates, exactly? The position of a joint is a set of three values: X, Y, and Z. The X, Y, and Z values are measured relative to the 3D Cartesian system. More specifically:

- X – The horizontal coordinate

- Y – The vertical coordinate

- Z – The depth coordinate

If you don't remember the Cartesian system from your high school math class, don't worry. Figure 6-5 demonstrates a sphere within the 3D space.

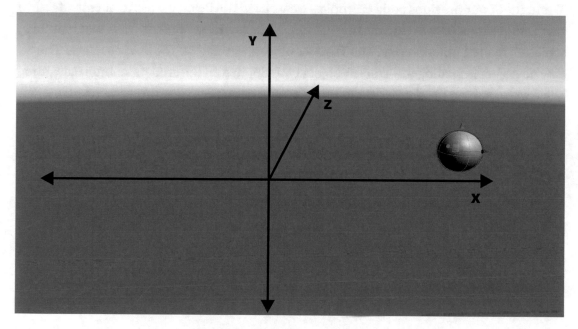

Figure 6-5. *The position of a joint in the 3D Cartesian system*

The reference point (0, 0, 0) of the axis is the Kinect itself. Horizontal (X) and vertical (Y) values can be positive or negative. As we've learned in Chapter 5, the depth (Z) axis has no negative values. Kinect can only see in front of it, not behind!

The coordinates of a joint are given in millimeters, but most of the time, you'll need to convert them to meters to use them in Unity3D.

Acquiring Body Data

You have a solid understanding of the mathematical concepts behind the Azure Kinect skeleton tracking system. Enough theory is enough, though! It's time to write some C# code, access the joints, and visualize them in a friendly 3D user interface.

Launch Unity3D and create a new 3D scene. Add an empty GameObject into the scene and attach it a new C# script. I've named it Azure_Kinect_BodyTracking.

Tracker Initialization

Throughout our previous code examples, we've used the Device class to access the raw data streams. The Body Tracking SDK introduces a new Tracker class that handles skeleton-related functionality. The Tracker objects depend on the Device. How? The Device object is feeding the Tracker object with depth and infrared data. Internally, the Tracker is passing the depth data to the AI neural network and gathers the results.

First, let's import the proper namespaces for both SDKs:

```
using Microsoft.Azure.Kinect.Sensor;
using Microsoft.Azure.Kinect.BodyTracking;
```

We can now declare the two object references:

```
private Device _device;
private Tracker _tracker;
```

Do not forget to add a reference to the configuration options class we had created in Chapter 2.

```
[SerializeField] private KinectConfiguration _configuration;
```

In the Start() method, we shall initialize the Device object in exactly the same way as we did in the previous examples. No changes, no surprises. The Tracker object is initialized based on the device calibration.

```
private void Start()
{
    _device = Device.Open();

    _device.StartCameras(new DeviceConfiguration
    {
        /* Specify the configuration properties */
        /* similarly to the previous chapters */
    });

    _tracker = Tracker.Create(_device.GetCalibration(), new
    TrackerConfiguration());
}
```

Did you notice the second parameter in the `Tracker.Create()` method? As you understand, the Tracker has its own set of configuration rules. Exploring this further, we see there are three tracking configuration options:

- AI model path
- Tracker processing mode
- Sensor orientation

The ModelPath option specifies the path of the Machine Learning model to use. Remember there are two models available: dnn_model_2_0_op11.onnx and dnn_model_2_0_lite_op11.onnx. In terms of skeleton tracking, the first one is 5% more accurate, but the second is two times faster. It makes sense to have the lighter model as our default.

The `TrackerProcessingMode` option specifies whether the AI will run on the CPU or the GPU. By default, it runs on the GPU because graphics cards are optimized for Machine Learning calculations. If you select the CPU mode, performance will drop significantly, so stick to the GPU mode instead.

The `SensorOrientation` option specifies how the sensor is positioned. You can use Kinect horizontally, rotated clockwise, anticlockwise, or upside down. Throughout the book, we'll be using the default device orientation. However, if your project could benefit from Kinect's portrait orientation, just update that setting and you are all set. In the following, you can see how to initialize the Tracker with different settings:

```
_tracker = Tracker.Create(_device.GetCalibration(), new
TrackerConfiguration
{
    ModelPath = "dnn_model_2_0_lite_op11.onnx",
    ProcessingMode = TrackerProcessingMode.Gpu,
    SensorOrientation = SensorOrientation.Clockwise90
});
```

Since I like being consistent, I updated the `KinectConfiguration` Unity class to expose the Body Tracking options in the Editor.

```
// KinectConfiguration.cs class

[SerializeField] private string _modelPath = "dnn_model_2_0_lite_
op11.onnx";
```

113

```
[SerializeField]
private TrackerProcessingMode _trackerProcessingMode =
TrackerProcessingMode.Gpu;
[SerializeField]
private SensorOrientation _sensorOrientation = SensorOrientation.Default;
```

Subsequently, we can initialize the Tracker directly in Unity3D, as shown in Figure 6-6, by assigning the corresponding properties of the KinectConfiguration class.

```
_tracker = Tracker.Create(_device.GetCalibration(), new
TrackerConfiguration
{
    ModelPath = _configuration.ModelPath,
    ProcessingMode = _configuration.TrackerProcessingMode,
    SensorOrientation = _configuration.SensorOrientation
});
```

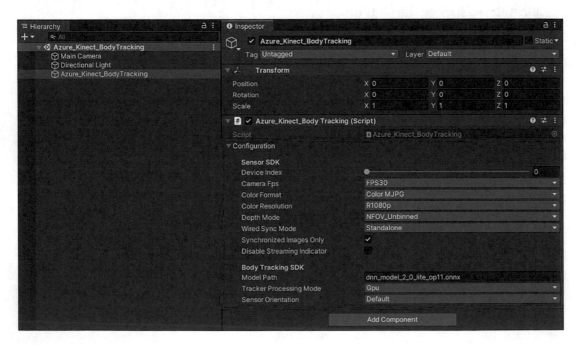

Figure 6-6. *Azure Kinect configuration options for body tracking*

Tracker Update

Remember that the Tracker needs the raw sensor data to infer the positions of the joints? Let's get to the Update() method and acquire the latest capture. We'll then feed that capture to the Tracker by using the EnqueCapture() method. EnqueCapture() adds the capture to an internal queue structure for processing. After getting a few captures, the Tracker will pop a result in the form of a Frame class.

```
private void Update()
{
    using (Capture capture = _device.GetCapture())
    {
        _tracker.EnqueueCapture(capture);

        using (Frame frame = _tracker.PopResult(TimeSpan.Zero, false))
        {
            // Work with the body frame here.
        }
    }
}
```

The PopResult() method accepts two arguments. The first argument specifies how long the Tracker should wait before checking the queue for a frame (timeout). We define a timeout of zero to avoid blocking the whole process. The second parameter specifies whether the method should throw an exception when the timeout is reached, and no data is available. If it's true, PopResult() will throw an exception. On the other hand, if we set it to false, the method will return a null frame. For now, we shall suppress the exception and simply check for null frames before accessing the skeleton information.

In the next chapter, we will explore a more performant way of accessing body data and handling such situations.

Constructing Body Objects

So we have the body-tracking results encapsulated as a Frame object. How can we access the individual skeletons? Simple: The Frame object allows us to loop through the available skeletons.

- To acquire a body skeleton object, we call the GetBodySkeleton() method.

- To read its unique identifier, we call the GetBodyId() method.

- Subsequently, to access the joint members, we need to call the GetJoint() method of the desired Skeleton object.

The following code loops into the bodies, captures their IDs, and displays the position of the Head, Neck, and Pelvis joints.

```
if (frame != null)
{
    for (uint i = 0; i < frame.NumberOfBodies; i++)
    {
        uint id = frame.GetBodyId(i);
        Skeleton skeleton = frame.GetBodySkeleton(i);

        Joint head = skeleton.GetJoint(JointId.Head);
        Joint neck = skeleton.GetJoint(JointId.Neck);
        Joint pelvis = skeleton.GetJoint(JointId.Pelvis);

        Debug.Log($"Head position: {head.Position}");
        Debug.Log($"Neck position: {neck.Position}");
        Debug.Log($"Pelvis position: {pelvis.Position}");
    }
}
```

Tracker Release

When finished, remember that we always need to release the resources we created. That's a crucial step to avoid memory leaks and allow the application to close smoothly. In Unity's OnDestroy() method, call the Shutdown() method to stop tracking bodies and the Dispose() method to release the Tracker.

```
private void OnDestroy()
{
    _tracker?.Shutdown();
    _tracker?.Dispose();

    _device?.StopCameras();
    _device?.Dispose();
}
```

And there you have it! That's exactly how you access the coordinates of the human body joints. Overall, it's pretty straightforward. Now, let's visualize the skeleton data by constructing a stick figure in Unity3D.

Displaying Body Data in Unity3D

Kinect tracks 32 human body joints. To create an intuitive visualization, we need to know the relations between them. Referring to Figure 6-4, you can see that each joint is connected to one or more others. For example, the left shoulder is connected to the left elbow, while the left elbow is connected to the left wrist. It makes sense to recreate that bone-like structure.

Doing so in Unity3D would require two very primitive objects: cubes and lines. Obviously, cubes will represent the joints, while lines will represent their connections.

Create a new class in Unity3D and name it Stickman. The Stickman instance shall contain an array of Transform objects for the cubes and another array of LineRenderer objects for the bones.

```
public class Stickman : MonoBehaviour
{
    [SerializeField] private Transform[] _cubes;
    [SerializeField] private LineRenderer[] _lines;
}
```

Back to the Editor, go on and create a container with 32 cubes and 32 lines. For reusability purposes, I have exported the container as a Prefab and placed it into the Resources folder of the project.

117

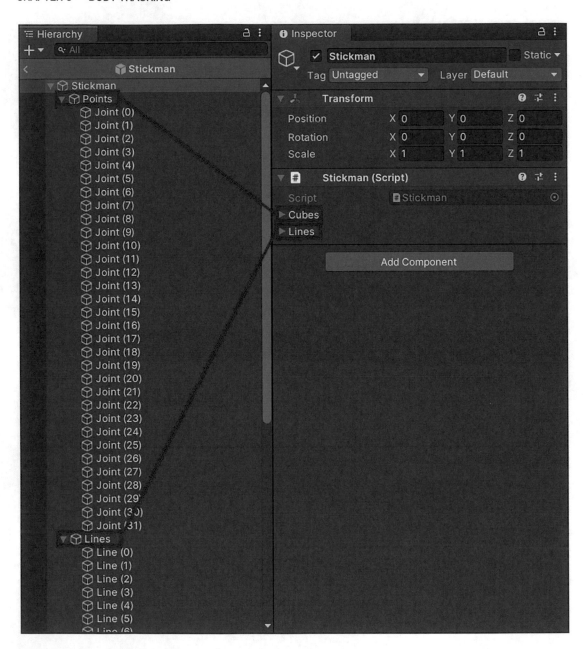

Figure 6-7. *A stick figure in Unity3D. We are using Cubes to represent the joints and Line Renderers to connect them together*

The Stickman class should explicitly specify the connections between the joints. A handy data structure to hold such kind of data would be an array of tuples. Each tuple specifies which joints should connect (e.g., Head with Neck, Neck with Chest, etc.). You can create your own connections by modifying that array. For now, I'm going to follow the bone structure in Figure 6-4. The core functionality of the Stickman class is straightforward:

- Each cube is assigned the position of the corresponding joint.

- Each line is assigned the positions of the corresponding bone.

Keep in mind that, as we learned in Chapter 5, Kinect stores 3D data in millimeters. Unity3D is using meters, so we have to divide each millimeter value by 1000.

Also, be careful with the native C# `Vector3` and `Quaternion` structures. Both are parts of the `System.Numerics` namespace; thus, we need to convert them to Unity3D's `Vector3` and `Quaternion` equivalents.

Here is the complete Stickman class:

```
public class Stickman : MonoBehaviour
{
    [SerializeField] private Transform[] _cubes;
    [SerializeField] private LineRenderer[] _lines;

    private readonly Tuple<JointId, JointId>[] _bones =
    {
        Tuple.Create(JointId.EarLeft, JointId.EyeLeft),
        Tuple.Create(JointId.EyeLeft, JointId.Nose),
        Tuple.Create(JointId.Nose, JointId.EyeRight),
        Tuple.Create(JointId.EyeRight, JointId.EarRight),
        Tuple.Create(JointId.Nose, JointId.Head),
        Tuple.Create(JointId.Head, JointId.Neck),
        Tuple.Create(JointId.Neck, JointId.SpineChest),
        Tuple.Create(JointId.Neck, JointId.ClavicleLeft),
        Tuple.Create(JointId.Neck, JointId.ClavicleRight),
        Tuple.Create(JointId.ClavicleLeft, JointId.ShoulderLeft),
        Tuple.Create(JointId.ClavicleRight, JointId.ShoulderRight),
```

```
        Tuple.Create(JointId.ClavicleRight, JointId.ShoulderRight),
        Tuple.Create(JointId.ShoulderLeft, JointId.ElbowLeft),
        Tuple.Create(JointId.ShoulderRight, JointId.ElbowRight),
        Tuple.Create(JointId.ElbowLeft, JointId.WristLeft),
        Tuple.Create(JointId.ElbowRight, JointId.WristRight),
        Tuple.Create(JointId.WristLeft, JointId.HandLeft),
        Tuple.Create(JointId.WristRight, JointId.HandRight),
        Tuple.Create(JointId.HandLeft, JointId.HandTipLeft),
        Tuple.Create(JointId.HandRight, JointId.HandTipRight),
        Tuple.Create(JointId.HandLeft, JointId.ThumbLeft),
        Tuple.Create(JointId.HandRight, JointId.ThumbRight),
        Tuple.Create(JointId.SpineChest, JointId.SpineNavel),
        Tuple.Create(JointId.SpineNavel, JointId.Pelvis),
        Tuple.Create(JointId.Pelvis, JointId.HipLeft),
        Tuple.Create(JointId.Pelvis, JointId.HipRight),
        Tuple.Create(JointId.HipLeft, JointId.KneeLeft),
        Tuple.Create(JointId.HipRight, JointId.KneeRight),
        Tuple.Create(JointId.KneeLeft, JointId.AnkleLeft),
        Tuple.Create(JointId.KneeRight, JointId.AnkleRight),
        Tuple.Create(JointId.AnkleLeft, JointId.FootLeft),
        Tuple.Create(JointId.AnkleRight, JointId.FootRight),
    };

public void Load(Skeleton body)
{
    // Joints/Cubes
    for (int i = 0; i < _cubes.Length; i++)
    {
        Joint joint = body.GetJoint((JointId) i);

        Vector3 position = new Vector3(joint.Position.X / 1000.0f,
        -joint.Position.Y / 1000.0f, joint.Position.Z / 1000.0f);

        _cubes[i].position = position;
    }
```

```
        // Bones/Lines
        for (int i = 0; i < _bones.Length; i++)
        {
            Joint joint1 = body.GetJoint(_bones[i].Item1);
            Joint joint2 = body.GetJoint(_bones[i].Item2);

            Vector3 position1 = new Vector3(joint1.Position.X / 1000.0f,
            -joint1.Position.Y / 1000.0f, joint1.Position.Z / 1000.0f);
            Vector3 position2 = new Vector3(joint2.Position.X / 1000.0f,
            -joint2.Position.Y / 1000.0f, joint2.Position.Z / 1000.0f);

            _lines[i].SetPosition(0, position1);
            _lines[i].SetPosition(1, position2);
        }
    }
}
```

Did you notice that we inverted the sign of the Y coordinate? That's because Y is mirrored compared to Unity's coordinate system, so we negate it to avoid having the skeleton upside down.

Back to our main script (Azure_Kinect_BodyTracking.cs), we will create a list of Stickman objects and update the list dynamically, based on the available skeletons. We destroy and recreate the list whenever the number of skeletons changes. This way, we avoid instantiating new prefabs on every frame. It's a smart move that gains a little bit of performance.

```
private List<Stickman> _stickmen = new List<Stickman>();

private void UpdateStickmen(List<Skeleton> skeletons)
{
    if (skeletons == null) return;

    if (_stickmen.Count != skeletons.Count)
    {
        foreach (Stickman stickman in _stickmen)
        {
            Destroy(stickman.gameObject);
        }

        _stickmen.Clear();
```

121

```
    foreach (Skeleton body in skeletons)
    {
        Stickman stickman = (Instantiate(Resources.Load("Stickman")) as
        GameObject)?.GetComponent<Stickman>();
        _stickmen.Add(stickman);
    }
}

for (int i = 0; i < skeletons.Count; i++)
{
    _stickmen[i].Load(skeletons[i]);
}
}
```

Finally, we need to modify the Update() method and call the UpdateStickmen() one. All we need to do is create a list of Skeleton objects and pass that list to the Stickman visuals.

```
if (frame != null)
{
    List<Skeleton> skeletons = new List<Skeleton>();

    for (uint i = 0; i < frame.NumberOfBodies; i++)
    {
        Skeleton skeleton = frame.GetBodySkeleton(i);

        skeletons.Add(skeleton);
    }

    UpdateStickmen(skeletons);
}
```

And there you have it! Our first body-tracking application is ready. Hit the Run button to see it in action. Stand in front of the sensor and check the stick figures that start filling the space. Move around, sit down, jump, squat, and the assigned Stickman will follow you precisely.

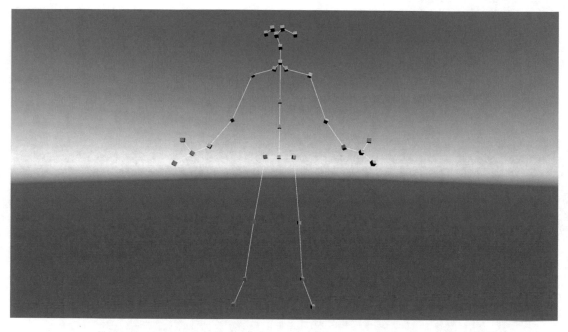

Figure 6-8. *A human skeleton in the 3D space – front view. The person is facing Kinect directly*

Now, try something else. Open the Scene window in Unity3D and use your mouse to rotate the view. Even if you stand facing the camera straight on, you can see precisely how your skeleton looks from the side view! Play around with different camera positions. Alternative angles can provide a ton of useful information to particular applications. For example, using the side view, you can gather insights about a person's posture – all that without having to actually look at the person from the side!

Figure 6-9. *The same human skeleton in side view. The person is still facing Kinect in front view, though! We are only moving Unity's scene camera*

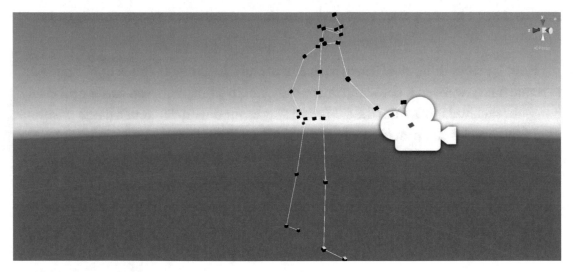

Figure 6-10. *The same human skeleton from the back*

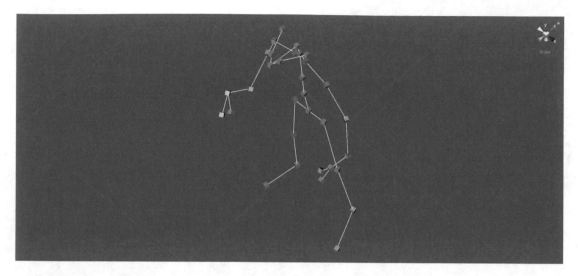

Figure 6-11. *Once again, the same skeleton, this time from an overhead view*

Key Points

In this chapter, we explored the Azure Kinect Body Tracking SDK. We've learned how to set up a `Tracker` object and feed it with `Device` data. Then, we acquired the IDs and joints of the available skeletons and constructed a stick-figure visualization to display the bodies on screen. The key takeaways are the following:

- The `Tracker` instance is serving skeleton frames whenever they are available.

- Each skeleton frame includes information about bodies and their joints.

- Each body has a unique identifier, as well as a collection of joints.

- Each joint contains an ID, Confidence Level, Position, and Quaternion properties.

Moving forward, we are going to apply a few key performance improvements and stream color, depth, and skeleton data in a background thread.

PART III

The Magic

CHAPTER 7

Streaming Data in the Background

Up to this point, we have learned how to stream data from the Kinect device. We fully understand how to properly open the cameras and acquire color, depth, body, and IMU information.

In our very first approach, we used Unity's Update() method to check for data. Even though this way is easy to illustrate and does not harm rapid prototyping, it is also quite problematic in real-world scenarios. Why? Because we are blocking Unity's main thread as we wait for new frames. Let's assume that you have selected the 30 FPS option in your Kinect settings. Calling the GetCapture() method would give you a set of data every 33 milliseconds. Until the data are ready, the method would just wait idly.

On the other hand, Unity's Update() method is running literally whenever a new game/app frame is available. If your computer allows it, the Update() method may be called, for example, 120 times per second. That's a great frame rate that allows smoother graphics and flawless animations into your apps and games.

But guess what? If Kinect or any other equivalent sensor is blocking the main thread waiting for data, then you are limited to 30 frames per second! Bye-bye, smooth animation.

Run the demos we've created so far and check the **Statistics** panel of your project (Game view ➤ Stats), you'll notice that it took the CPU approximately 33 milliseconds to render one game frame!

© Vangos Pterneas 2022
V. Pterneas, *Mastering the Microsoft Kinect*, https://doi.org/10.1007/978-1-4842-8070-6_7

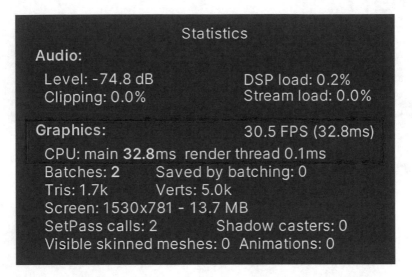

Figure 7-1. *Waiting for Kinect frames in the* Update() *method blocks the main thread and limits the game frame rate to about 30 FPS*

How are we supposed to solve this problem? Thankfully, our apps and games can use the power of multithreading to run various tasks concurrently. The C# language provides a solid toolset that allows us to accomplish multithreading tasks in an easy and straightforward way. We'll start by creating a data structure encapsulating the Kinect data we need.

Creating a Data Package

Let's create a structure that holds raw Kinect data. So far, we know we need the following types of data:

- A unique timestamp

- The temperature value

- A byte array for the color data

- A ushort array for the depth data

- A list of bodies

- The accelerometer and gyroscope vectors

Of course, Kinect will not always generate synchronized frames so that we may end up with empty data for some types. That's fine: we'll set the empty data structures to null. Here is a simple class that represents each data type as a simple C# property:

```
public class KinectData
{
    public DateTime Timestamp { get; set; }
    public float Temperature { get; set; }
    public byte[] Color { get; set; }
    public ushort[] Depth { get; set; }
    public ImuSample Imu { get; set; }
    public List<Body> Bodies { get; set; }
}
```

Creating the Streaming Class

To keep things intact, we will encapsulate all of the Kinect streaming functionality into a single class. That class will provide members and methods for starting, stopping, and getting data from the Kinect sensor. Moreover, it will expose a simple interface for interacting with the sensor without having to mess with the Device and Tracker objects explicitly.

So let's start building that class. At first, we need to declare a Device and a Tracker instance. Additionally, we need a reference to the data package class we created in the previous step. The data package member will hold the latest data we captured. Last but not least, we need a member that specifies whether the sensor is running. We'll be accessing that member from multiple threads, so we'll declare it as a volatile C# variable.

```
public class KinectSensor
{
    private Device _device;
    private Tracker _tracker;
    private KinectData _frameData;
    private volatile bool _isRunning;
    private readonly object _lock = new object();

    // Start, Stop, and streaming methods will follow.
}
```

The _lock object we declared will be used later on for thread safety reasons.

131

Starting and Stopping the Device

First, the easy stuff: a method that initializes the Device and Tracker objects with the proper configuration parameters and activates the cameras and the IMU. There we'll move the functionality we have already developed in the previous chapters. The following code performs the following:

- Checks for the number of connected Kinect devices

- Opens the Device

- Starts the cameras based on the specified configuration parameters

- Starts the accelerometer and gyroscope sensors

- Creates the Tracker instance based on the specified configuration parameters

- Sets the _isRunning variable to true only if the initialization process succeeds

```
public void Start(KinectConfiguration configuration = null)
{
    _isRunning = false;

    if (Device.GetInstalledCount() <= 0)
    {
        Debug.LogWarning("No Kinect devices available.");
        return;
    }

    if (configuration == null)
        configuration = new KinectConfiguration();

    try
    {
        _device = Device.Open(configuration.DeviceIndex);
```

```
    if (_device == null)
    {
        Debug.LogError($"Kinect sensor {configuration.DeviceIndex} is
        not available.");
        return;
    }

    _device.StartCameras(new DeviceConfiguration
    {
        CameraFPS = configuration.CameraFps,
        ColorFormat = configuration.ColorFormat,
        ColorResolution = configuration.ColorResolution,
        DepthMode = configuration.DepthMode,
        DisableStreamingIndicator = configuration.
        DisableStreamingIndicator,
        WiredSyncMode = configuration.WiredSyncMode,
        SynchronizedImagesOnly = configuration.SynchronizedImagesOnly
    });
    _device.StartImu();

    _tracker = Tracker.Create(_device.GetCalibration(), new
    TrackerConfiguration
    {
        ModelPath = configuration.ModelPath,
        ProcessingMode = configuration.TrackerProcessingMode,
        SensorOrientation = configuration.SensorOrientation
    });

    _isRunning = true;

    Stream();
}
catch (Exception e)
{
    Debug.LogError(e);
}
}
```

As you can see, the method ends by calling the Stream() function upon successful initialization. In case something unusual happens, we place everything into a try-catch block. If something goes wrong, the _isRunning variable will act as an insurance policy – it's set to true only after all operations have been successfully initialized. Lastly, we are calling the primary method of this process: Stream(). We are going to explore the functionality of Stream()very soon.

Before doing so, we'll create the Stop() method. Once again, we are copying the code from previous chapters to shut down the Tracker and close the Device cameras and IMU. We also set the _isRunning member to false.

```csharp
public void Stop()
{
    _isRunning = false;

    _tracker?.Shutdown();
    _tracker?.Dispose();

    _device?.StopCameras();
    _device?.StopImu();
    _device?.Dispose();
}
```

Moving forward, we will implement the Stream() method and acquire the Kinect data on a different thread.

Streaming Data in a Background Thread

C# comes with a bunch of goodies for managing threads. The simplest one is the Task. Run() method. Task.Run() is a way to execute code asynchronously. Whatever you write inside the Run block is queued to run on a different thread.

```csharp
Task.Run(() => { /* Long-running operation here */ }
```

C# is usually choosing a thread from the thread pool that's assigned to your application. On our end, we are going to place a loop that checks for and captures Kinect data. That's the place to get the color and depth data, as well as the skeleton objects.

Of course, we need to keep asking for data in a loop until the Stop() method is called. So we are going to run the data capture code in a while statement. The _ isRunning member will be used as a flag to stop the execution and exit the thread.

Whenever we capture new data, we'll assign them to the _frameData object we created before. Without further ado, here is the complete streaming method:

```
private void Stream()
{
    Task.Run(() =>
    {
        try
        {
            while (_isRunning)
            {
                using (Capture capture = _device.GetCapture())
                using (Image color = capture.Color)
                using (Image depth = capture.Depth)
                {
                    DateTime timestamp = DateTime.FromBinary(depth.
                    SystemTimestampNsec);
                    byte[] colorData = MemoryMarshal.AsBytes(color.Memory.
                    Span).ToArray();
                    ushort[] depthData = MemoryMarshal.Cast<byte,
                    ushort>(depth.Memory.Span).ToArray();
                    List<Skeleton> bodyData = null;
                    ImuSample imuSample = _device.GetImuSample();

                    _tracker.EnqueueCapture(capture);

                    using (Frame bodyFrame = _tracker.PopResult(TimeSpan.
                    Zero, false))
                    {
                        if (bodyFrame != null && bodyFrame.
                        NumberOfBodies > 0)
                        {
                            bodyData = new List<Skeleton>();
```

```
                    for (uint i = 0; i < bodyFrame.
                    NumberOfBodies; i++)
                    {
                        Skeleton skeleton = bodyFrame.
                        GetBodySkeleton(i);

                        bodyData.Add(skeleton);
                    }
                }
            }

            KinectData newData = new KinectData
            {
                Timestamp = timestamp,
                Temperature = capture.Temperature,
                Color = colorData,
                Depth = depthData,
                BodyIndex = bodyIndexData,
                Bodies = bodyData,
                Imu = imuSample
            };

            lock (_lock)
            {
                KinectData temp = newData;
                _frameData = temp;
            }
        }
    }
    catch
    {
        // Tried to access disposed objects. Ignore.
    }
});
}
```

Most of the Stream() method includes no new information. We've just grouped everything we have been doing over the past four chapters. When we bundled everything into a KinectData structure, we used the lock statement to assign the structure into the private _frameData member. The lock statement is a safety handle: it ensures that no other threads can access our precious _frameData object as long as we assign its value. Upon exiting the lock block, other threads can access the object safely.

In multithreading scenarios, always use lock blocks to restrict access only to the thread that's modifying the objects. External threads will not be able to alter it.

Finally, we placed the code inside a try-catch block to avoid surprises and keep the application running no matter what.

Updating the Main Thread

We have intentionally declared the Steam() method as private. We don't want other processes to access it and mess with the background thread. Instead, we'll be responsible for returning the latest data packages to external callers. So how are external classes supposed to interact with our streaming service?

Keep in mind that outside processes, such as the MonoBehaviour scripts we've been using, have no idea how often Kinect is ready to serve new frames. As a result, they may ask for the same frame multiple times. It's our job to capture the latest data and maintain them in the _frameData variable. We know that each data package has a unique timestamp we can use to specify whether we have already served that package before. In case we did, then our method will return null. Otherwise, it will return the _frameData object.

First, we'll declare a DateTime member to store the last timestamp we served:

```
private DateTime _lastRequestedTimestamp;
```

Then, we'll implement the Update() method, starting with some checks. If the background thread is not running, or if the _frameData object is null, then we return null. Otherwise, Update() is comparing the timestamps and returns either

- Null if the same frame was requested before

- The _frameData object if the frame was never requested

The return code is crucial, and we need to ensure that no other threads can modify the _frameData value. That's precisely why we are placing the return statement inside a lock statement block. In the following, you can see the complete Update() method.[1]

```
public KinectData Update()
{
    if (!_isRunning) return null;
    if (_frameData == null) return null;

    lock (_lock)
    {
        if (_frameData.Timestamp == _lastRequestedTimestamp)
            return null;

        _lastRequestedTimestamp = _frameData.Timestamp;

        return _frameData;
    }
}
```

Using the KinectSensor Class

After doing all this hard work, it's time for my favorite part: using the background streaming provider in our Unity scenes. Remember the MonoBehaviour scripts we created in the previous chapters? Check how tidy and clean our code becomes. All we need to do is

- Create a read-only KinectSensor object

- Initialize the KinectSensor object with the specified configuration inside the Start() method

- Grab a data package inside the Update() method

- Stop the camera in the OnDestroy() method

---

[1] Do not confuse this Update() method with Unity's reserved Update() one. This is not a MonoBehaviour class, so I'm allowed to name it as I like. However, if you prefer to use a different name, such as GetData() or AcquireLatestFrame(), feel free to do so!

Here is an example script:

```
public class KinectSensorDemo : MonoBehaviour
{
    [SerializeField] private KinectConfiguration _configuration;

    private readonly KinectSensor _kinect = new KinectSensor();

    private void Start()
    {
        _kinect.Start(_configuration);
    }

    private void Update()
    {
        if (!_kinect.IsRunning) return;

        KinectData frameData = _kinect.Update();
    }

    private void OnDestroy()
    {
        _kinect.Stop();
    }
}
```

Now, that's amazingly simple! We've reduced our Kinect dependencies to a single KinectSensor member and a couple of method calls.

But would it be more efficient compared to our initial approach? Once again, run the application and open the Statistics panel (Game view ➤ Stats). Notice that the main thread is now free and running at full speed. Kudos!

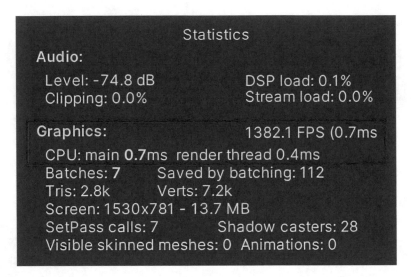

Figure 7-2. *While streaming Kinect data from a background thread, the main thread remains free*

From now on, we'll be using our new `KinectSensor` class to acquire Kinect data throughout the book. Moreover, we are going to enhance it with additional functionality in the next chapters.

In case you would like to experiment with the background streaming approach, roll back to Chapters 4 to 6 and update the source code using the `KinectSensor` class. After that, check the code repository of this book and compare your solution.

Our fresh approach is not only more efficient, but it's also more convenient since all of the Kinect-related code is fully reusable. Plus, we avoid polluting the main `MonoBehaviour` Unity classes with repeated code, saving a ton of keystrokes.

Key Points

In this chapter, we implemented an essential operation in terms of software performance and efficiency. Instead of capturing Kinect data in the main thread of our Unity application, we created a background streaming provider. As a result, Kinect is no longer blocking the execution of the main thread, and we can use it for other application-specific operations, such as animations and business logic.

The background streaming provider includes methods for starting the cameras, stopping the cameras, processing frames, and passing the latest frame to the main thread when requested.

In the next chapters, we will use and extend that streaming provider to accommodate new use-case scenarios.

CHAPTER 8

Coordinate Mapping

In the previous chapters, we've seen that the video and depth cameras provide two-dimensional screen-friendly outputs, while the joint data are referenced in the three-dimensional physical world. A video frame is an image with X and Y data measured in pixels, while a skeleton frame includes X, Y, and Z values measured in meters. How is that possible, and what does it mean for the way you should approach your Kinect development process? In this chapter, we will demystify Kinect's coordinate spaces and transform between 2D and 3D.

It's natural to feel overwhelmed by all those coordinate systems or even think that you need a solid mathematical background to understand them. Well, even though an experience in maths would be of help, the core concepts are pretty intuitive as long as you familiarize yourself with them. Mastering the different coordinate systems will allow you to develop more sophisticated applications with a higher level of control. Not only will you know how to visualize different types of data, but you'll also be able to combine data from other coordinate spaces.

For example, let's assume you are developing an intelligent fitness application measuring the elbow flexion angle for performing dumbbell curls. Your app should display the video camera feed; calculate the angle between the shoulder, elbow, and wrist joints; and visualize the angle on top of the RGB color image. The app should look like Figure 8-1. In this case, the flexion angle is measured in degrees, calculated using the three-dimensional (X, Y, Z) physical coordinates of three joints. The joint centers and their respective connecting lines are drawn using the two-dimensional (X, Y) pixel locations.

© Vangos Pterneas 2022
V. Pterneas, *Mastering the Microsoft Kinect*, https://doi.org/10.1007/978-1-4842-8070-6_8

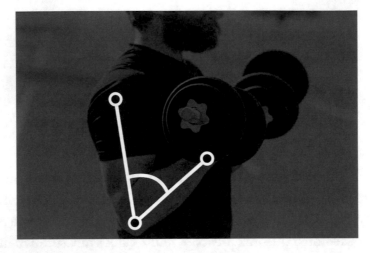

Figure 8-1. *A real-world example of combining information from multiple coordinate spaces. In this case, it measures the elbow flexion angle*[1]

Spoiler alert: We will see exactly how to develop such a cool fitness application in Chapter 10.

Coordinate Systems

Before exploring the different Kinect coordinate systems, let's start with the one everything is based upon: the Cartesian coordinate system.

The Cartesian coordinate system is the most widely used method of representing points within a particular space area. Here's a quick reminder of your high school math class. We are using perpendicular lines, also called axes, to specify the planes of motion. As a convention, a horizontal axis is called X, while a vertical axis is called Y. X and Y define a two-dimensional plane. Add a third perpendicular axis, called Z, and we've got a three-dimensional system, where every single point is uniquely described as a pair of distances – one distance from each axis. The distances are called **coordinates** and can be positive, negative, or zero.

In computer science, we are using variations of the Cartesian system to represent different types of data. Let's recap what coordinate systems Kinect uses.

---

[1] Image credit: `https://pexels.com`

2D Coordinates

Whenever we display a picture on a computer screen, we visualize it on the X and Y axes. Moreover, it's convenient *not* to have negative values. That's why, as we've already seen, the color and depth data are represented as positive values within a rectangular plane.

- The reference point [0, 0] is at the top-left corner.

- Horizontal values increase from left to right.

- Vertical values increase from top to bottom.

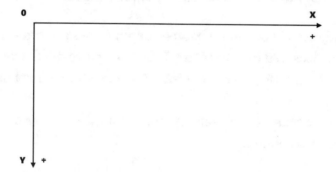

Figure 8-2. *A 2D coordinate system, with X and Y axes*

The maximum horizontal value is equal to the width of the color or depth frame (e.g., 1920), and the maximum vertical value is the height of the frame (e.g., 1080). As a result, the pair [152, 428] is a valid point, while [250, -404] is not.

3D Coordinates

When it comes to the physical 3D space, Kinect uses itself as the reference point [0, 0, 0].

- The reference point [0, 0, 0] is the middle of the space, and it's Kinect itself.

- Horizontal values may be positive or negative. They increase from left to right.

- Vertical values may also be positive or negative. They increase from top to bottom.

- Depth values can only be positive. They increase as we move farther from the camera.

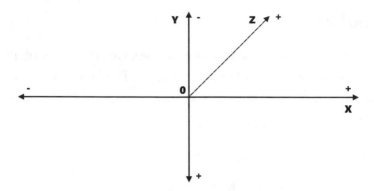

Figure 8-3. *A 3D coordinate system with X, Y, and Z axes*

As we've already seen in previous chapters, depth values can never be negative. Since everything is measured in terms of the Kinect, negative depth would indicate points behind the camera. Obviously, that is impossible unless Kinect had a 360-degree field of view.

Now that we know what we are dealing with, we can see how we can transform from one coordinate space to another.

Coordinate Mapping

Have you ever wondered why there are so many coordinate systems in the first place? That's simply because Kinect has two cameras: a video camera and a depth sensor.[2] As you can see in Figure 8-4, the color and depth cameras are not perfectly aligned. That implies they see the world from a slightly different angle. Moreover, they have different resolutions and lenses: the depth lens can see a narrow or a wide area of the physical space, while the video lens can see an HD or a 4K image.

---

[2] Moreover, the IMU (accelerometer and gyroscope) also specifies its own 3D coordinate system.

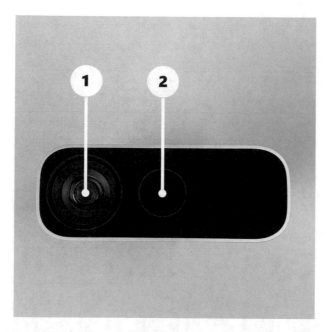

Figure 8-4. *The Azure Kinect color (1) and depth (2) cameras*

If you pick a point within the color video frame, you cannot assume its coordinates would correspond to the same point of the depth frame! Let me give you an example of this: assuming you have specified a color resolution of 1920×1080 and a depth resolution of 640×576. The first thing you notice is that the color array is larger than the depth array. As a result, a color point with coordinates of, for example, [840, 712] is outside the range of the depth array. Even the color point [150, 200] does not correspond to the depth point [150, 200].

Figure 8-5. *A color and a depth frame captured at the same time*

As you can see in Figure 8-6, if you overlay the two frame types, their points are not aligned.

Figure 8-6. *By default, the color and depth frames are not aligned*

That's normal, but how could we overcome this problem? Thankfully, it's possible to align the frames if we know the special characteristics of the cameras. Such unique features include

- The viewing angle of each camera

- The distance between the cameras within the Kinect bundle

- The type and distortion of the lenses

- The resolution of the cameras

You may encounter these parameters as **intrinsics** and **extrinsics**. For now, all you need to know is that such parameters describe the hardware characteristics and the relations between the cameras. If we knew these parameters, we could apply mathematical transformations and map the data on a 1:1 basis. Thankfully, we won't need to do any maths. The Kinect SDK is already aware of the camera features and exposes a simple C# API for us to use. To transform between the various coordinate spaces, we will create a new coordinate mapping class and use the proper SDK methods.

Coordinate Transformations

Kinect exposes its coordinate mapping interface via the `Calibration` class. As you'll shortly see, its class methods involve the `System.Numerics.Vector2` and `Vector3` data structures. So on my end, I'm going to create a class named `CoordinateMapper` to encapsulate this functionality and interact directly with Unity's equivalent vector structures. The coordinate mapping class will support the following transformations, of which we'll create the appropriate methods:

- World (3D) to Color (2D)

- World (3D) to Depth (2D)

- Color (2D) to World (3D)

- Depth (2D) to World (3D)

- Color (2D) to Depth (2D)

- Depth (2D) to Color (2D)

149

Why is Depth considered 2D and not 3D? When talking about coordinate spaces, we refer to how each frame type is presenting its data. Depth data is an array of distances. The X and Y values are pixel coordinates and not physical units; only the **value** of each X/Y pair is a physical distance measurement. The coordinates per se are pixel units. We need to convert them into their respective physical equivalents – and that's exactly what the Kinect SDK is doing internally.

Here's the initial interface of the class:

```
public class CoordinateMapper
{
    private Calibration _calibration;

    public CoordinateMapper(Calibration calibration)
    {
        _calibration = calibration;
    }
    public Vector2 MapWorldToColor(Vector3 point3D)
    {
        // TODO
    }
    public Vector2 MapWorldToDepth(Vector3 point3D)
    {
        // TODO
    }

    public Vector2 MapColorToWorld(Vector2 point2D)
    {
        // TODO
    }

    public Vector2 MapDepthToWorld(Vector2 point2D, float depth)
    {
        // TODO
    }
```

```
public Vector2 MapColorToDepth(Vector2 pointColor)
{
    // TODO
}
public Vector2 MapDepthToColor(Vector2 pointDepth, float depth)
{
    // TODO
}
}
```

Let's implement those methods one by one.

World to Color

We'll start with the most common transformation: 3D world points to 2D color points. A human body joint is a pair of X, Y, and Z values in the 3D space. In Chapter 6, we visualized the joints in Unity's 3D view by using those values as is. To overlay the points on top of the color frame, however, we need to transform the physical values into pixels. The Calibration class exposes a method named TransformTo2D, which converts a point from the 3D space to a specified 2D space. Here's an example:

```
var input = new System.Numerics.Vector3(-697.4f, -557.6, 1591.2); // Units
are millimeters
var output = _calibration.TransformTo2D(
        input,
        CalibrationDeviceType.Depth, CalibrationDeviceType.Color);

if (output.HasValue)
{
    Debug.Log($"{output.Value.X:N0}x{output.Value.Y:N0}");
    // Prints something like: 540x320
}
```

The TransformTo2D method accepts three arguments:

- An object of type Vector3, holding the X, Y, and Z values

- A source camera type

- The destination camera type

In our case, the source is set to the **Depth** camera because 3D values are generated solely by the depth sensor. The destination camera is, obviously, the **Color** one.

Notice we are using the System.Numerics.Vector3 class instead of the equivalent UnityEngine.Vector3. Internally, the Kinect SDK uses the standard .NET structures to be compatible with engines other than Unity3D. For convenience reasons, I'm converting the System.Numerics vector to a Unity vector, so we can seamlessly use it in our user interface.

So let's now create a more generic method inside the CoordinateMapper class to accept any 3D point:

```
public Vector2 MapWorldToColor(Vector3 point3D)
{
    Vector2 point2D = Vector2.zero;

    try
    {
        var input = new System.Numerics.Vector3(point3D.x, point3D.y,
        point3D.z);
        var output = _calibration.TransformTo2D(input, CalibrationDevice
        Type.Depth, CalibrationDeviceType.Color);

        if (output.HasValue)
        {
            point2D.Set(output.Value.X, output.Value.Y);
        }
    }
    catch
    {
        // Color or depth camera is turned off.
    }

    return point2D;
}
```

The method is accepting a Unity vector object and converts it to its equivalent Numerics vector. Then, it's passing that vector to the transformation method. If the transformation went smooth, the output structure would have a non-null value. In that case, we create and return a new Unity vector structure. Otherwise, we return the zero vector. Notice that we wrapped everything into a try-catch statement. Why's that? Sometimes, the video camera or the depth sensor might be turned off.[3] If that's the case, the transformation function will fail and throw a runtime exception! Catching the exception and returning a zero vector will allow the application to proceed smoothly. You are encouraged to print a diagnostic message based on your use-case scenario.

World to Depth

The process for converting 3D world coordinates to 2D depth coordinates would be identical to what we previously demonstrated. The only difference is that we'll transform from the same (Depth) device type and not the Color one.

```
public Vector2 MapWorldToDepth(Vector3 point3D)
{
    Vector2 point2D = Vector2.zero;

    try
    {
        var input = new System.Numerics.Vector3(point3D.x, point3D.y,
        point3D.z);
        var output = _calibration.TransformTo2D(input, CalibrationDevice
        Type.Depth, CalibrationDeviceType.Depth);

        if (output.HasValue)
        {
            point2D.Set(output.Value.X, output.Value.Y);
        }
    }
    catch
    {
        // Depth camera is turned off.
    }

    return point2D;
}
```

---

[3] Refer to Chapter 3.

Color to World

Doing the opposite task is a little trickier. When transforming from 2D to 3D, the Calibration class needs to know the depth of the pixel to covert. But as we know, color pixels do not have a depth value. How could we solve that problem? It turns out we have to map the whole video image to the depth camera. This way, we'll create a buffy depth array with a size equal to the color one! Doing so, we need to use another Kinect utility class, called `Transformation`. The Transformation class can map whole frames to other camera types.[4] However, it requires the latest Kinect `Capture` instance as its input. As a result, we have to update our `CoordinateMapper` class accordingly and feed it with Capture object inputs.

First, we'll add two private members:

```
private readonly Transformation _transformation;
private Capture _capture;
```

The transformation should be created once, right into the constructor:

```
public CoordinateMapper(Calibration calibration)
{
    _calibration = calibration;
    _transformation = _calibration.CreateTransformation();
}
```

Secondly, we'll update the Capture with the newest instance:

```
public void Update(Capture capture)
{
    _capture = capture;
}
```

We can now create depth images with the size of the color frames:

```
public Image DepthToColor =>
    _transformation.DepthImageToColorCamera(_capture);
```

---

[4] The Transformation class also allows the generation of point clouds.

154

Last but not least, the Image is a disposable object, so we need to release its internal resources when done:

```
public void Dispose()
{
    DepthToColor?.Dispose();
}
```

Now that we've gone through this process, we can find the depth of the desired color pixel! First, we'll access the underlying ushort depth data array. Remember, this is an array of **distances** with the size of a color image frame.

Finding the depth value is a mathematical calculation: given (a) the size of a one-dimensional array and (b) the X and Y coordinates of a point, the depth index is calculated by the following formula:[5]

$$index = point.Y * width + point.X$$

Here's the complete color-to-world method implementation:

```
public Vector3 MapColorToWorld(Vector2 point2D)
{
    ushort[] depthData = MemoryMarshal.Cast<byte, ushort>(DepthToColor.
    Memory.Span).ToArray();

    int index = (int)point2D.y * DepthToColor.WidthPixels + (int)point2D.x;
    ushort depth = depthData[index];

    Vector3 point3D = Vector3.zero;

    try
    {
        var input = new System.Numerics.Vector2(point2D.x, point2D.y);
        var output = _calibration.TransformTo3D(input, depth,
        CalibrationDeviceType.Color, CalibrationDeviceType.Depth);
```

---

[5] Keep this formula in mind whenever you know the X and Y coordinates of a point and you want to find its index within a 1D array.

155

```
        if (output.HasValue)
        {
            point3D.Set(output.Value.X, output.Value.Y, output.Value.Z);
        }
    }
    catch
    {
        // Color or depth camera is turned off.
    }

    return point3D;
}
```

As you understand, the preceding method is more expensive in terms of computational resources, so use with care. Even though converting from color to world is not a typical scenario, we are going to make heavy use of it in Chapter 16.

Depth to World

The remaining coordinate transformation methods are way more straightforward. No need to map whole frames – just use the Calibration methods with the appropriate arguments. As a subsequent task, we'll map a depth point to the 3D world space. A depth point is a pair of X and Y pixels with a millimeter value. The Calibration class is internally transforming the X and Y pixel coordinates to their millimeter equivalents.

```
public Vector3 MapDepthToWorld(Vector2 point2D, float depth)
{
    Vector3 point3D = Vector3.zero;

    try
    {
        var input = new System.Numerics.Vector2(point2D.x, point2D.y);
        var output = _calibration.TransformTo3D(input, depth,
        CalibrationDeviceType.Color,
            CalibrationDeviceType.Depth);
```

```
        if (output.HasValue)
        {
            point3D.Set(output.Value.X, output.Value.Y, output.Value.Z);
        }
    }
    catch
    {
        // Depth camera is turned off.
    }

    return point3D;
}
```

Color to Depth

When mapping a color pixel to the depth space, we, once again, need to know its depth value. Consequently, we'll need to apply the same frame transformation, as we did when converting color to world. This method will return the 2D X and Y pixel coordinates of the depth point and not the 3D world position.

```
public Vector3 MapColorToWorld(Vector2 point2D)
{
    ushort[] depthData = MemoryMarshal.Cast<byte, ushort>(DepthToColor.
    Memory.Span).ToArray();

    int index = (int)point2D.y * DepthToColor.WidthPixels + (int)point2D.x;
    ushort depth = depthData[index];

    Vector3 point3D = Vector3.zero;

    try
    {
        var input = new System.Numerics.Vector2(point2D.x, point2D.y);
        var output = _calibration.TransformTo3D(input, depth,
        CalibrationDeviceType.Color, CalibrationDeviceType.Depth);
```

```
        if (output.HasValue)
        {
            point3D.Set(output.Value.X, output.Value.Y, output.Value.Z);
        }
    }
    catch
    {
        // Ignore - Color is turned off
    }

    return point3D;
}
```

Depth to Color

Lastly, we'll implement a depth-to-color mapping method. This one is much simpler and only relies on the Calibration utility.

```
public Vector2 MapDepthToColor(Vector2 pointDepth, float depth)
{
    Vector2 pointColor = Vector2.zero;

    try
    {
        var input = new System.Numerics.Vector2(pointDepth.x,
        pointDepth.y);
        var output = _calibration.TransformTo2D(input, depth, Calibration
        DeviceType.Depth, CalibrationDeviceType.Color);

        if (output.HasValue)
        {
            pointColor.Set(output.Value.X, output.Value.Y);
        }
    }
```

```
catch
{
    // Color or Depth camera is turned off.
}

return pointColor;
}
```

Using the Coordinate Mapper Class

For ease of access, let's add the CoordinateMapper as a member of our KinectSensor class:

```
public CoordinateMapper CoordinateMapper { get; internal set; }
```

We'll initialize the coordinate mapper in the Start method, right after starting the cameras:

```
Calibration calibration = _device.GetCalibration();
CoordinateMapper = new CoordinateMapper(calibration);
```

To get rid of any unmanaged resources, we'll dispose the mapper in the Stop method:

```
CoordinateMapper?.Dispose();
```

Whenever a new Capture is available, we'll feed it to the mapper:

```
using (Capture capture = _device.GetCapture())
using (Image color = capture.Color)
using (Image depth = capture.Depth)
{
    CoordinateMapper.Update(capture);
    // Rest of code here…
}
```

Using the CoordinateMapper is neat and easy. As an example, loop into all of the tracked bodies, and acquire the screen coordinates of their joints. Assuming you've captured the skeleton body data as shown in Chapter 6, here's how you can transform them to 2D:

```
if (frameData != null)
{
    List<Skeleton> bodies = frameData.Bodies;

    if (bodies != null)
    {
        foreach (var body in bodies)
        {
            for (int i = 0; i < (int)JointId.Count; i++)
            {
                var joint = body.GetJoint(i);
                var position3D = new Vector3(joint.Position.X, joint.
                Position.Y, joint.Position.Z);

                var position2D = _kinect.CoordinateMapper.
                MapWorldToColor(position3D));

                Debug.Log($"3D position: {position3D}");
                Debug.Log($"2D position: {position2D}");
            }
        }
    }
}
```

Add some nice-looking dots and lines, and you'll have the result of Figure 8-7.

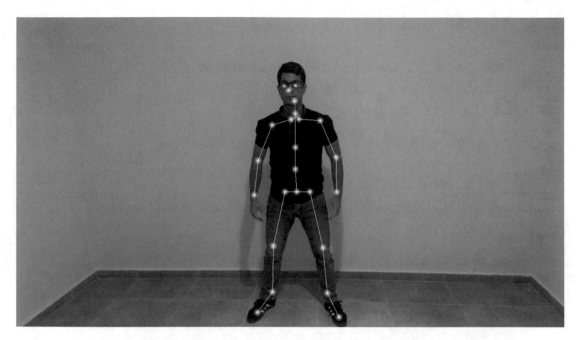

Figure 8-7. *Mapping the 3D joint coordinates to 2D color coordinates*

Here's some homework for the brave devs. Use your knowledge from Chapters 4 and 6 to draw the joints on top of a Unity Canvas. In Chapter 4, we drew the video frame on a Unity Image component. In Chapter 6, we acquired the 3D body joint coordinates. Since you are now aware of how to transform the joint coordinates to pixel values, add a few circular graphics to your Unity project and update their anchorPosition according to the coordinate mapping results. Then, compare your solution with the example I've included in the source code of this book.

The Complete Coordinate Mapper Class

The CoordinateMapper class is a handy tool that will come in handy in later chapters. For your reference, find the entire class in the following. We'll be using its methods throughout the book from now on.

```csharp
public class CoordinateMapper : IDisposable
{
    private readonly Transformation _transformation;
    private Calibration _calibration;
    private Capture _capture;

    public CoordinateMapper(Calibration calibration)
    {
        _calibration = calibration;
        _transformation = _calibration.CreateTransformation();
    }

    public void Update(Capture capture)
    {
        _capture = capture;
    }

    public Image DepthToColor =>
        _transformation.DepthImageToColorCamera(_capture);

    public void Dispose()
    {
        DepthToColor?.Dispose();
    }

    public Vector2 MapWorldToColor(Vector3 point3D)
    {
        Vector2 point2D = Vector2.zero;

        try
        {
            var input = new System.Numerics.Vector3(point3D.x, point3D.y,
            point3D.z);
            var output = _calibration.TransformTo2D(input,
            CalibrationDeviceType.Depth, CalibrationDeviceType.Color);
```

```
        if (output.HasValue)
        {
            point2D.Set(output.Value.X, output.Value.Y);
        }
    }
    catch
    {
    }

    return point2D;
}

public Vector2 MapWorldToDepth(Vector3 point3D)
{
    Vector2 point2D = Vector2.zero;

    try
    {
        var input = new System.Numerics.Vector3(point3D.x, point3D.y,
        point3D.z);
        var output = _calibration.TransformTo2D(input, Calibration
        DeviceType.Depth, CalibrationDeviceType.Depth);

        if (output.HasValue)
        {
            point2D.Set(output.Value.X, output.Value.Y);
        }
    }
    catch
    {
    }

    return point2D;
}
```

```
public Vector3 MapColorToWorld(Vector2 point2D)
{
    ushort[] depthData = MemoryMarshal.Cast<byte, ushort>(DepthToColor.
    Memory.Span).ToArray();

    int index = (int)point2D.y * DepthToColor.WidthPixels + (int)
    point2D.x;
    ushort depth = depthData[index];

    Vector3 point3D = Vector3.zero;

    try
    {
        var input = new System.Numerics.Vector2(point2D.x, point2D.y);
        var output = _calibration.TransformTo3D(input, depth,
        CalibrationDeviceType.Color, CalibrationDeviceType.Depth);

        if (output.HasValue)
        {
            point3D.Set(output.Value.X, output.Value.Y, output.Value.Z);
        }
    }
    catch
    {
    }

    return point3D;
}

public Vector3 MapDepthToWorld(Vector2 point2D, float depth)
{
    Vector3 point3D = Vector3.zero;

    try
    {
        var input = new System.Numerics.Vector2(point2D.x, point2D.y);
        var output = _calibration.TransformTo3D(input, depth,
        CalibrationDeviceType.Color,
            CalibrationDeviceType.Depth);
```

```
        if (output.HasValue)
        {
            point3D.Set(output.Value.X, output.Value.Y, output.Value.Z);
        }
    }
    catch
    {
    }

    return point3D;
}

public Vector2 MapColorToDepth(Vector2 pointColor)
{
    ushort[] depthData = MemoryMarshal.Cast<byte, ushort>(DepthToColor.
    Memory.Span).ToArray();

    int index = (int)pointColor.y * DepthToColor.WidthPixels + (int)
    pointColor.x;
    ushort depth = depthData[index];

    Vector2 pointDepth = Vector2.zero;

    try
    {
        var input = new System.Numerics.Vector2(pointColor.x,
        pointColor.y);
        var output = _calibration.TransformTo2D(input, depth,
        CalibrationDeviceType.Color, CalibrationDeviceType.Depth);

        if (output.HasValue)
        {
            pointDepth.Set(output.Value.X, output.Value.Y);
        }
    }
    catch
    {
    }
```

```
        return pointDepth;
    }

    public Vector2 MapDepthToColor(Vector2 pointDepth, float depth)
    {
        Vector2 pointColor = Vector2.zero;

        try
        {
            var input = new System.Numerics.Vector2(pointDepth.x,
            pointDepth.y);
            var output = _calibration.TransformTo2D(input, depth,
            CalibrationDeviceType.Depth, CalibrationDeviceType.Color);

            if (output.HasValue)
            {
                pointColor.Set(output.Value.X, output.Value.Y);
            }
        }
        catch
        {
        }

        return pointColor;
    }
}
```

Key Points

In this chapter, we explored the different Kinect coordinate systems. We used the Azure Kinect SDK's calibration methods to transform between the color, depth, and physical spaces. We also implemented a handy coordinate mapping class to assist with further development. Before moving forward, keep in mind the following:

- Coordinate mapping is the process of transforming the location of a point from one space to another.

- Color and depth frames provide 2D screen data values measured in pixels.

- World positions are physical 3D locations measured in pixels.

- We can transform between the color, depth, and physical world space by calling the appropriate methods of the `Calibration` instance.

- When we need to map a whole frame, we use the `Transformation` class to create the appropriate frame representation.

CHAPTER 9

Augmented Reality: Removing the Background of the Users

Augmented Reality has become a familiar term mostly due to mobile devices. Major smartphone manufacturers such as Apple and Google are making huge breakthroughs in the ways our everyday devices understand the environment. Augmented Reality is the result of enhancing the physical world with digital content, such as 3D objects, interactable elements, and so on. Usually, people see such enhanced versions of reality through headsets like Microsoft's HoloLens or through the screens of their phones. Few people attribute the wide use of AI to Kinect, which has been the device that made AR mainstream.

Launched in 2010, the original Kinect for XBOX was able to detect human bodies. To do so, it needed to extract the human shape from the camera environment. It could then overlay 3D objects on top of the body or move the body into an entirely new area, like a sports court or a rainforest! There was one problem preventing people from calling that reality "augmented," though: Kinect, just like the XBOX, has been using the TV monitor to output the data. Unlike headsets and smartphones, a TV cannot move around, and it feels less personal and disconnected.

The truth is the basic principles of Augmented Reality are the same regardless of the means you have chosen. In this chapter, we are going to see how we can blend digital objects into the camera space. You can also apply that knowledge to different cases and technologies. Understanding how to use a Kinect is knowledge you can easily transfer to similar domains, such as mobile development or HoloLens prototyping.

© Vangos Pterneas 2022
V. Pterneas, *Mastering the Microsoft Kinect*, https://doi.org/10.1007/978-1-4842-8070-6_9

Figure 9-1. *The cutout of a person in front of a solid green color*

Mixing the Physical and the Digital Worlds

You can use a HoloLens headset to project 3D dinosaurs in front of your eyes. That's cool. You know what's even cooler? Being able to interact with the dinosaurs and even fight with them using your bare fists. Even without the immersiveness of a headset, Kinect can help us implement the latter scenario. To do so, we'll need to subtract the players from their surroundings and replace the physical environment with a jungle (well, I assume jungle was a thing 65 million years ago). We'll then add dinosaurs into the scene, and after that, your game developer inspiration will do the rest. Let's get started!

Background Removal

Background removal, also referred to as "background segmentation" or "green-screen effect," is the process of identifying the points within an image that belong to the body of a person and removing all other points, such as background elements and nearby objects. We can break down the segmentation process in the following steps:

- Kinect captures synchronized color and depth frames.

- The SDK is processing the infrared image of the depth frame to identify the points that belong to the visible people.

- Then, the Body Tracking SDK is producing a special frame type, called Body Index map.

- The Sensor SDK is aligning the color and depth frames, so we have an 1-1 pixel mapping. Now, each depth pixel has an equivalent color one.

- Lastly, we select the pixels that are marked as "human" and delete all others.

Figure 9-2 shows a capture from my Kinect's video camera. As you can see, apart from the person, there are nearby objects (such as my chair), faraway objects, walls, light, etc.

Figure 9-2. *The Azure Kinect color frame: a person, a nearby object, and background walls*

The equivalent capture of the depth camera is shown in Figure 9-3. Again, you can easily identify the shape of the person, the chair, and the walls.

Figure 9-3. *The corresponding depth frame*

Aligning the color and depth frames produces a new RGB image that is precisely mapped to the depth visualization, as shown in Figure 9-4.

Figure 9-4. *The result of the depth-to-color alignment*

Why is alignment important? Because the Kinect SDK is using **only** the depth frame to identify the human body data! That means it detects a human within the 640×576 depth array, not the 1920×1080 RGB image. For most use-case scenarios, though, we need the RGB visualization. So we have to manually align the frames using the coordinate mapping methods we saw in Chapter 9.

Figure 9-5 displays the result of the background removal process.

Figure 9-5.   *The result of removing nearby objects and background elements, leaving only the pixels that belong to a person*

By extracting only the body pixels, we can replace the original environment with a different color, a different picture, video, or even 3D objects! That's the definition of an **immersive** experience. In this chapter, we are going to develop a simple Unity3D game that will immerse the player in entirely different surroundings. Figure 9-4 shows the result of the segmentation process.

Some people would likely assume that Kinect is applying a dummy depth filter: "if distance of wrist is Z, then keep all pixels within that range plus or minus a few inches." However, this assumption is wrong. Unlike what you might initially think, Kinect is not filtering the points this way. Instead, the whole segmentation process is built right into the Machine Learning model. In my case, a simple depth filter would not be able to distinguish between points that belong to the forearm and points that belong to the chair, since they all have similar distance from the camera. AI is about more sophisticated solutions than traditional computer vision techniques: the Deep Neural Network is intentionally trained to recognize whether a point is part of a body or not. That includes the complete silhouette of a person, not just the skeleton joints. So how can we use the segmentation process programmatically? It all starts with the Body Index map.

The Body Index Map

The shape of a human silhouette is quite abstract: unlike common object tracking techniques, we cannot assume it's going to be rectangular. Moreover, humans tend to move their limbs, bend in different directions, and take unpredictable poses. Remember: Human skeleton tracking and body segmentation is entirely done on the depth/infrared frames. The RGB color images are not required. That's exactly why the SDK provides the silhouette in terms of the depth frame and not the color one.

The Body Index map is a very simple array that marks whether a particular pixel belongs to a body. Here's how it works:

- If a pixel is not part of a person, its value is going to be 255 (background pixel).

- If a pixel is part of a person, it's value is going to be 1, 2, 3, etc.

So if two people stand in front of the camera, the pixels of the first person would have the value "1", while the pixels of the second person would have the value "2". The pixels are encoded as a one-dimensional array of size depth width × depth height. Figure 9-6 shows a simplified visualization of a Body Index array.

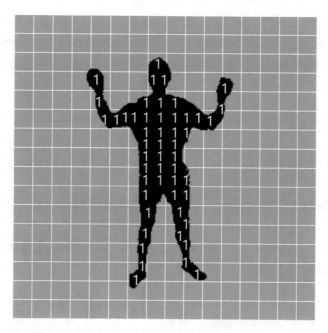

Figure 9-6. *Simplified structure of a Body Index map*

We access the Body Index map via the body frame reference, similar to what we did with the skeleton data. To expose the map to our common interface, we'll need to add a new byte array reference into the KinectData structure we created in the previous chapters.

```
public class KinectData
{
    public DateTime Timestamp { get; set; }
    public float Temperature { get; set; }
    public byte[] Color { get; set; }
    public ushort[] Depth { get; set; }
    public List<Skeleton> Bodies { get; set; }
    public byte[] BodyIndex { get; set; }
}
```

Foo

Move on in the Stream method of your KinectSensor class and declare a new array element, alongside the skeleton list:

```
byte[] bodyIndexData = null;
```

As we've seen, the Body Index byte array has the exact same size with the depth data array. To fill the array, navigate to body frame acquisition and capture a new Image named BodyIndexMap. The process is straightforward, identical to the color frame acquisition:

```
using (Frame bodyFrame = _tracker.PopResult(TimeSpan.Zero, false))
{
    if (bodyFrame != null)
    {
        using (Image bodyIndex = bodyFrame.BodyIndexMap)
        {
            bodyIndexData = MemoryMarshal.AsBytes(bodyIndex.Memory.Span).
            ToArray();
        }

        // Acquire skeleton data here...
    }
}
```

We can then assign the value of the BodyIndex property:

```
KinectData newData = new KinectData
{
    Timestamp = timestamp,
    Temperature = capture.Temperature,
    Color = colorData,
    Depth = depthData,
    ColorToDepth = colorToDepthData,
    Bodies = bodyData,
    BodyIndex = bodyIndexData
};
```

Whenever we acquire a new Kinect frame, we can loop into the BodyIndex member and check whether each pixel belongs to a human body. If so, we are going to paint that pixel black; otherwise, we'll paint it transparent. In the following, you'll find a very simple method to colorize the Body Index frame. We've added a second array of type Color32. The array is filled with RGBA values depending on each Body Index pixel.

The Frame class includes a handy constant member named BodyIndexMapBackground. It's hard-coded to 255 and indicates that a pixel belongs to the background and not the humans.

```
byte[] bodyIndex = frameData.BodyIndex;

if (bodyIndex != null)
{
    Color32[] colors = new Color32[bodyIndex.Length];

    for (int i = 0; i < bodyIndex.Length; i++)
    {
        if (bodyIndex[i] != Frame.BodyIndexMapBackground)
        {
            // This pixel belongs to a human
            colors[i] = Color.black;
        }
        else
        {
            // This pixel belongs to the background
            colors[i] = Color.clear;
        }
    }
}
```

As an exercise to you, feed that Color32 array to a Unity Texture2D object, then pass it to an Image UI component, and get a result similar with Figure 9-7. We expect to see black silhouettes of the active users.

Figure 9-7. *A visualization of the body index frame*

So that's the first part of the process. We have successfully identified the silhouettes of the people and colorized the corresponding pixels. We've got a quite spooky visualization, so let's make it a little better. Moving forward, we'll use our coordinate mapping knowledge to find the RGB points of the tracked users.

Mapping Color to Depth

The Azure Kinect device bundles an RGB video camera alongside a depth sensor. As we've seen in the previous chapter, these cameras are discrete yet not isolated: we can use the Sensor SDK to transform between the RGB and depth coordinates. That's exactly what we are going to do now in order to acquire the color point equivalents.

How's that possible? Let's assume that your device is streaming 1080p color frames (1920×1080) and NFOV depth frames (640×576). The color resolution is much higher compared to the depth resolution. Internally, the Kinect SDK will create a new image type at a 640×576 resolution and will populate it by selecting the appropriate pixels from the 1920×1080 frame. So we, the developers, will end up with a frame type with RGB information at a lower resolution.

Note that the new frame type will not have any depth data. The depth information will still persist as part of the original depth frame. The color-to-depth frame will only hold pixel (RGB) values. As we'll see, those color values are perfectly aligned with the depth values!

The first step of this process is to update our configuration settings. The depth and color cameras stream frames at slightly different time points. Since we need to map whole frames, we need to instruct the sensor to provide synchronized frames only. As a result, we need to set the SynchronizedImagesOnly to true, or check the corresponding field in the handy Unity Editor configuration element.

Moreover, after we map the color and depth frames, we need to loop within the color pixels and keep only the ones that belong to the players – just like we did in the earlier code snippet. As a result, it will come in handy to set the ColorFormat member to BGRA32. The BGRA32 array is uncompressed, and we can easily search it in a simple for-loop.

Figure 9-8 shows the updated configuration options of our Unity scene.

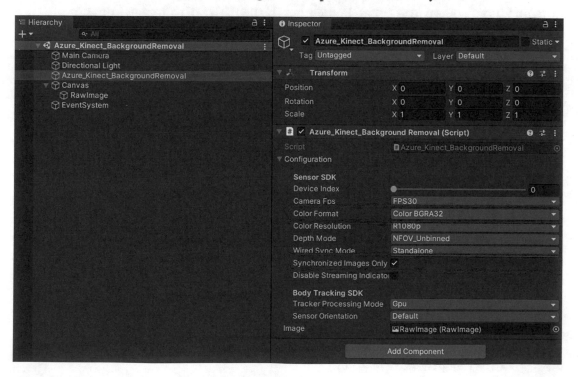

Figure 9-8. *Color-to-depth mapping settings*

Back to our data streaming code, we add a new property to the existing `KinectData` class. We already have the raw arrays of the color (byte) and depth (ushort) frames. The new property would hold the color data after the color-to-depth transformation process. I've named it `ColorToDepth`, and it's of BGRA array type. BGRA is the name of a Kinect SDK structure for representing pixels with red, green, blue, and alpha transparency.

```
public class KinectData
{
    public DateTime Timestamp { get; set; }
    public float Temperature { get; set; }
    public byte[] Color { get; set; }
    public ushort[] Depth { get; set; }
    public List<Skeleton> Bodies { get; set; }
    public byte[] BodyIndex { get; set; }
    public BGRA[] ColorToDepth { get; set; }
}
```

The Azure Kinect SDK already provides methods for transforming a frame from one input source to another. Remember the `DepthToColor` image from our `CoordinateMapper` class? That property mapped the whole depth frame to its corresponding color frame. This time, we need to do the opposite and create a new property applying the `ColorImageToDepthCamera` transformation.

```
public Image ColorToDepth =>
    _transformation.ColorImageToDepthCamera(_capture);
```

Do not forget to dispose the new Image when finished.

```
public void Dispose()
{
    ColorToDepth?.Dispose();
    DepthToColor?.Dispose();
}
```

Then, we need to call that new property from inside our `KinectSensor` class. Move to the streaming method of the `KinectSensor` and add a reference to the new BGRA array:

```
BGRA[] colorToDepthData = null;
```

As the device receives frames, populate the array by calling the ColorToDepth property. The syntax is familiar to that of previous chapters.

```
using (Image colorToDepthImage = CoordinateMapper.ColorToDepth)
{
    colorToDepthData = colorToDepthImage.GetPixels<BGRA>().ToArray();
}
```

Remember to assign the `ColorToDepth` property of the `KinectData`. This way, the frame data bundle that we'll serve to Unity3D will have all of the required information.

```
KinectData newData = new KinectData
{
    Timestamp = timestamp,
    Temperature = capture.Temperature,
    Color = colorData,
    Depth = depthData,
    Bodies = bodyData,
    BodyIndex = bodyIndexData,
    ColorToDepth = colorToDepthData
};
```

If you now display the BGRA data to Unity3D, you'll end up with an image similar to Figure 9-9. Don't worry – we are going to write the C# code in a minute. Notice the rectangular shape of the frame? That's because the colorized data are aligned to the depth frame.

Figure 9-9. *Color-to-depth frame alignment*

It's time for our background removal demo in Unity3D. All we need to do is combine the knowledge we already have. I assume you have already applied the required configuration settings (BGRA32 color format and Synchronized Images Only) in Unity3D. Now, add a new C# script and add a RawImage UI and a Texture2D element to display the coordinate mapping results. Moreover, since we are dealing with BGRA data, add a Unity Color32 array to hold those values.

In the Start() method, open the sensor, create the texture, and initialize the Color32 array. Keep in mind that you need to provide the resolution (width and height) of the depth frame. Moreover, we'll change the texture format to BGRA32, so we can properly deal with the BGRA data.

```
public class Azure_Kinect_BackgroundRemoval : MonoBehaviour
{
    [SerializeField] private KinectConfiguration _configuration;
    [SerializeField] private RawImage _image;

    private Texture2D _texture;
    private Color32[] _colors;

    private readonly KinectSensor _kinect = new KinectSensor();
```

```
    private void Start()
    {
        _kinect.Start(_configuration);

        int depthWidth = 640;
        int depthHeight = 576;

        _texture = new Texture2D(depthWidth, depthHeight, TextureFormat.
        BGRA32, false);
        _colors = new Color32[depthWidth * depthHeight];
        _image.texture = _texture;
    }

    private void OnDestroy()
    {
        _kinect.Stop();
    }
}
```

Let's move to the Update() method, where magic happens. Here's what we are going to do:

- First, we'll capture the ColorToDepth and BodyIndex arrays. Remember that both arrays have exactly the same size!

- Then, we'll loop into those arrays to examine their pixels one by one.

- For each pixel, we are going to check whether it belongs to a human body.

- If the pixel belongs to a body, we'll copy the B, G, R, and A values to our Color32 array.

- If the pixel does not belong to a body, we'll simply set the equivalent Color32 value to transparent.

Here's the code to accomplish all this.

```
private void Update()
{
    if (!_kinect.IsRunning) return;

    KinectData frameData = _kinect.Update();
```

```
    if (frameData != null)
    {
        BGRA[] colorToDepth = frameData.ColorToDepth;
        byte[] bodyIndex = frameData.BodyIndex;

        if (colorToDepth != null && bodyIndex != null)
        {
            for (int i = 0; i < bodyIndex.Length; i++)
            {
                if (bodyIndex[i] != Frame.BodyIndexMapBackground) // 255
                {
                    // This pixel belongs to a human
                    // Use the colors of the human body
                    _colors[i].b = colorToDepth[i].B;
                    _colors[i].g = colorToDepth[i].G;
                    _colors[i].r = colorToDepth[i].R;
                    _colors[i].a = colorToDepth[i].A;
                }
                else
                {
                    // This pixel belongs to the background
                    _colors[i] = Color.clear;
                }
            }

            _texture.SetPixels32(_colors);
            _texture.Apply();
        }
    }
}
```

Figure 9-10 displays the end result of the alignment with body segmentation.

Figure 9-10. *The color frame mapped to the depth frame with background removal*

The players can now move to a totally virtual space. That's a cool AR experience, isn't it? But we are not going to stop there. Unity makes it extremely easy to add more visual elements and enhance the experience. Moreover, adding digital background elements would make the pixelated contours look much smoother.

A Background Removal Game in Unity3D

As a device tailored to immersive experiences, Kinect has been used in museum exhibitions to attract young (and older) visitors. So let's say you are developing an app for a Museum of Natural History. Instead of simply showing dinosaurs, why not place the visitors right inside the Jurassic period (only safer)?

I've grabbed some cool royalty-free illustrations of a T-Rex and a prehistoric forest. They are simple PNG files, shown in Figures 9-11 and 9-12.

Figure 9-11. *The cutout of a prehistoric T-Rex[1]*

---

[1] Image credit: Stephen Leonardi from Unsplash (`https://unsplash.com/photos/1rTOJHpEsCo`).

Figure 9-12. *A beautiful image of a forest jungle we'll use as background in our game*[2]

Back to the Unity Editor, drag and drop the images into your **Assets** folder and set their **Texture Type** to **Sprite (2D and UI)**. After importing the images to your project, add two Image UI elements into the background removal scene. Remember to place them both **behind** the RawImage element we created earlier. Finally, set their source to the forest and T-Rex illustrations. The result is displayed in Figure 9-13.

---

[2] Image credit: Dave Hoefler from Unsplash (https://unsplash.com/photos/vW1TR9cBcSg).

Figure 9-13. *The assembled scene of our game*

Pretty simple, right? I dare you click the Play button! Notice how the person is immersed into the prehistoric digital forest, directly facing the T-Rex.

Figure 9-14. *T-Rex vs. Human. An immersive experience made with Kinect!*

For further development, replace the T-Rex illustration with an animated 3D model. You can even make the dinosaur chase the tracked people and create all kinds of interactive immersive games.

Key Points

In this chapter, we dived into one of the most stunning Kinect features: background removal. To accomplish this, we needed a new frame type, called Body Index. Body Index is an array of integer values, each one specifying whether a particular pixel belongs to a human body. To segment the background of the users, follow these steps:

- Synchronize the color and depth streams.

- Capture the Body Index frame type.

- Align the color frame to the depth frame.

- Loop into the Body Index frame and check its pixels one by one.

- Keep the pixels that belong to a human body and colorize them according to the aligned pixels.

CHAPTER 10

Motion Analysis

What do the fitness icon Arnold Schwarzenegger and the ancient Greek mathematician Euclid have in common? The answer is geometry. Euclid laid the foundations of geometry, allowing scientists to objectively measure the relative positions of objects. Arnold, consciously or not, used geometry to apply proper form during his training and maximize his muscle gains: when doing squats, he ensured his back did not bend forward; when doing bicep curls, he ensured his forearms traveled the whole range of motion.

In this chapter, we'll explore one of the emerging Kinect and motion capture markets: fitness. The fitness industry is exploding – and the recent pandemic has accelerated the adoption of intelligent applications that can help casual athletes get the most out of their workouts. Markerless skeleton tracking is the holy grail of fitness, and companies Tempo and eGym, to name a few, are already providing AI-assisted training via sophisticated apps. Those applications are acting as personal trainers, constantly measuring and evaluating the athletes' movements at the blink of an eye. Let's see how to develop one such app.

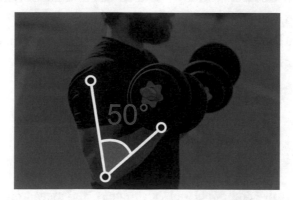

Figure 10-1. *Measuring the angle between the shoulder, elbow, and wrist joints to count bicep curls*

Motion Analysis

Before even diving deeper into the fitness waters, let's take a step back and examine what motion analysis is. After all, fitness involves many different practices, exercises, limb positions, and compound movements. **Motion analysis is the process of accurately detecting the human skeleton, measuring data, and providing feedback.**[1] I will break down each of these concepts so that you have a solid understanding of the primary principles and can develop your fitness and health-care apps by the end of the chapter.

1) Skeleton Data

Skeleton tracking is, well, the process of detecting the position of the human body joints. It's what Kinect has been perfecting since 2010. Using advanced Artificial Intelligence and Machine Learning, Kinect processes the color and depth data to segment the human bodies and estimate the 2D and 3D positions of their joints. This way, developers can track the movements of multiple people using a single Kinect camera.

In the past, similar tasks were extremely cumbersome: if someone wanted to track the position of the elbows, the subject should put on a wearable sensor. Then, a technician should properly attach the wearable to the subject while ensuring decent mobility. The sensor would then connect to a nearby computer and transmit data via wire or Bluetooth. Even though it was accurate, the process used to be slow and expensive. Plus, you needed to repeat the whole calibration process every time for each individual. Kinect provides a similar level of accuracy at a fraction of the cost, let alone how easy it is to set up and use.

In this chapter, we'll explore the relations of the Kinect skeleton data to acquire meaningful results for the users.

---

[1] Motion analysis may involve additional tools, techniques, and measurements. For example, wearable devices, such as smartwatches, heart-rate monitors, or even medical-grade equipment can be used to analyze the human motion. In this chapter, we are focusing on the capabilities of Kinect; thus, we only discuss markerless motion analysis. If your application involves more sophisticated data from different input sources, do not hesitate to use whatever would work best for your customers.

2) Measurements

Kinect is understanding the world in three dimensions and can simultaneously pay attention to multiple people – that's an amazingly focused personal trainer! From a technical standpoint, the three-dimensional joint positions are just tuples of X, Y, and Z coordinates we call **vectors**. However, we intuitively know that the human joints are connected. Using just the 3D coordinates along with the joint IDs, we can estimate the relationships between them. From now on, we'll be referring to these relationships as **measurements**. There are three types of measurements we can capture:

- Distances – How close or far are two or more joints? We'll see how to measure joint distances as physical values (meters, inches) and as percentages. For example, if you add the distance between the left hand, left elbow, left shoulder, right shoulder, right elbow, and right hand, you'll get the person's wingspan.[2]

- Angles – Three joints are forming an angle, with one of them being its corner. Angular measurements come in handy when measuring repetitions. For example, the angle between the shoulder, the elbow, and the wrist will indicate a bicep curl.

- Speed – How much distance did a joint travel during a specific amount of time? We'll use the joint positions of multiple frames to estimate how fast or slow someone is.

3) Feedback

No matter how good you are in software programming, it means nothing if the user is struggling to use your application. Measuring the human motion involves a lot of hard work on the developer's side. It's easy to assume that your job is done after doing the math, but nothing could be further from the truth. You need to provide meaningful feedback to your users and co-programmers. Feedback is part of user experience and usually goes underestimated. Here's why you need to care.

---

[2] Here's an exercise for you: Use this chapter to create an app that automatically measures the wingspan of basketball players.

Let's, again, assume your user (athlete) is doing bicep curls. Your application is measuring the angle between the shoulder, elbow, and wrist joints. During the motion, the angle would range between 180 degrees (fully extended arm) and 30 degrees (wrist close to chest), approximately. So you output this value and your app seems cool. When you notice that the athlete is struggling to lift the weights, you are tempted to instruct them "elbow angle should be greater than 90 degrees." It's easy to assume that the user knows what those numbers mean. Wrong! What the athlete truly cares about is some sort of plain and simple feedback like "move your wrist higher." As we've seen throughout the whole book, it's our job as software creators to hide all the non-essential complexity and provide human-friendly output.

Since this is a technical book, we are mostly focusing on doing the math and writing the code – both demanding tasks. In a real-world, scenario, though, you should strive to ensure that the end user is only seeing what's necessary. In the following examples, we are going to see exactly how to get from complex measurements to dead-simple feedback.

Without further ado, follow me to investigate the three measurement types: distances, angles, and speed.

Measuring Physical Distances

What is a physical distance? Our daily experience teaches us it's how far or close two objects are. Our brain is estimating distances all the time: it's measuring the distance between my foot and the stairs, the distance between my car and the front one, even the distance between my fingers and the keyboard, as I'm typing these lines. The brain is calculating these measurements subconsciously without giving it any profound thinking.[3] Can we use Kinect to mimic that ability? Of course, we can.

To do so, we need to define a "distance" in more strict terms. Here comes Euclid to provide the formal definition:

Euclidean distance between two points is the length of the shortest possible path between them.

---

[3] Someone could say that the human brain's CPU is running a "background thread."

So distance is the length of a straight-line segment between two points. To measure a distance, we need to know the coordinates of the points in every dimension. Thankfully, the Azure Kinect SDK is providing the coordinates of the human joints right out of the box! For simplicity reasons, let's begin with one dimension (X axis). In the one-dimensional space, our points only have a single coordinate: x_1 and x_2, respectively.

Figure 10-2. *The distance between two points in the 1D space*

Their distance is the absolute value of their subtraction:

$$d = |x_2 - x_1|$$

What is the equivalent formula in C#? Let's assume we have a Skeleton instance and we are interested in the shoulder joints:

```
var point1 = body.GetJoint(JointId.ShoulderLeft).Position;
var point2 = body.GetJoint(JointId.ShoulderRight).Position;
```

Check how easy it is to translate the preceding formula in C#:

```
float distance = Mathf.Abs(point2.X - point1.X);
```

In the two-dimensional space, our points now have two coordinates: (x_1, y_1) and (x_2, y_2). Measuring their distance becomes trickier, and we need to consult Pythagoras, another ancient Greek mathematician. As you can see in Figure 10-3, we can construct a right-angled triangle between with the point distance as the hypotenuse.

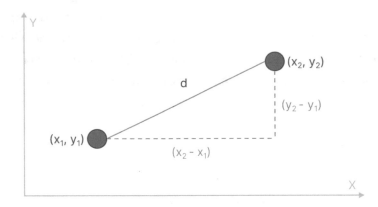

Figure 10-3. *The distance between two points in the 2D space*

According to the Pythagorean theorem,[4] the square root of the hypotenuse is equal to the sum of the squares of the other two sides:

$$d^2 = (x_2 - x_1)^2 + (y_2 - y_1)^2$$

So the distance would be equal to the square root of the aforementioned:

$$d = \sqrt{(x_2 - x_1)^2 + (y_2 - y_1)^2}$$

which, in turn, we'll translate in C#:

```
float distance = Mathf.Sqrt(
    (point2.X - point1.X) * (point2.X - point1.X) +
    (point2.Y - point1.Y) * (point2.Y - point1.Y));
```

Moving to the three-dimensional space, our points have three coordinates: (x_1, y_1, z_1) and (x_2, y_2, z_2). The good thing is the formula becomes no more complex! All we need to do is add the square of the third dimension (Z):

$$d = \sqrt{(x_2 - x_1)^2 + (y_2 - y_1)^2 + (z_2 - z_1)^2}$$

---

[4] You can refer to the Appendix of this book for a more thorough explanation. For now, you can just keep using the formula as is.

And in C#:

```
float distance = Mathf.Sqrt(
    (point2.X - point1.X) * (point2.X - point1.X) +
    (point2.Y - point1.Y) * (point2.Y - point1.Y) +
    (point2.Z - point1.Z) * (point2.Z - point1.Z));
```

Let's try to pour some real-world values in those numbers. I'm standing in front of my Kinect camera, and I'm reading the following numbers for the left and right shoulder joints:

- Left shoulder (point1): (0.17, -0.22, 2.05)

- Right shoulder (point2): (-0.19, -0.18, 2.12)

Applying the formula gives me the number 0.36, which is the distance of my shoulders in meters. I can replace the joint IDs from ShoulderLeft and ShoulerRight to, for example, AnkleLeft and AnkleRight to get the distance of my ankles or any other joint! Why not extract that formula into its own method?

```
public float Distance(Vector3 point1, Vector3 point2)
{
    return Mathf.Sqrt(
        (point2.X - point1.X) * (point2.X - point1.X) +
        (point2.Y - point1.Y) * (point2.Y - point1.Y) +
        (point2.Z - point1.Z) * (point2.Z - point1.Z));
}
```

The preceding method will come in handy as we are now going to evaluate a squat position!

Example: Evaluating a Squat

The squat is one of the most popular compound movements for building muscle. So no surprise most fitness classes have one form of squat or another in their routine. The most basic type of squat requires nothing but the person's weight, but you can also do it with dumbbells or a barbell. It's a very simple exercise, which requires the athlete to lower the hips down like sitting on an invisible chair. To avoid injuries, athletes should maintain proper form during the movement. That's where our Kinect-based trainer comes in.

Before starting the movement, athletes need to ensure that their feet are shoulder-width apart – that means the ankles should not be too close. Human personal trainers are estimating how far apart the athlete's feet are by simply looking at the person. How is the computer supposed to do the same thing? Let's put our math knowledge in action and teach it!

Figure 10-4. *The shoulder and ankle segments in the 3D space. When doing a squat, the second segment should be greater than the first one*

As it's obvious in Figure 10-4, we need to capture four joints (left/right shoulder, left/right ankle) and measure two distances: the shoulder and the ankle segments. I believe it's time to use the `Distance()` method we created earlier on (thank you, Pythagoras and Euclid!). In the following code, I'm assuming you have used your knowledge from Chapter 6 to capture a `Skeleton` object, named `body`. The code would be part of Unity's `Update()` method.

```
// 1. Capture the joints involved.
Vector3 shoulderLeft =
    body.GetJoint(JointId.ShoulderLeft).Position;
Vector3 shoulderRight =
    body.GetJoint(JointId.ShoulderRight).Position;
Vector3 ankleLeft =
    body.GetJoint(JointId.AnkleLeft).Position;
Vector3 ankleRight =
    body.GetJoint(JointId.AnkleRight).Position;
// 2. Measure the required distances.
float distShoulders = Distance(shoulderLeft, shoulderRight);
float distAnkles = Distance(ankleLeft, ankleRight);

// 3. Give feedback!
if (distShoulders > distAnkles)
{
    Debug.LogWarning("Move your feet further apart!");
}
else
{
    Debug.Log("Looking good!");
}
```

And there you have it! Our digital personal trainer can accurately evaluate proper form in real time. That was easy, right? Let's move to a different exercise and a different measurement type: angles.

Measuring Angles

The human body is a complex machine. Its joints are moving in different directions all the time – especially during a workout session. Measuring distances is only providing that much information. How about capturing more information regarding the relative movement of the joints? Assume you are doing the most common fitness exercise: a bicep curl: you are keeping your arm vertically straight while the forearm is moving up and down. Three key joints are involved: the shoulder, the elbow, and the wrist. During the curl, the only joint moving is the wrist. Sure, it's getting closer and farther to the shoulder, but what would that distance tell you? What distance is considered "good" or "bad"? What happens to people with bigger or smaller limbs?

It's apparent that we need a new measurement type. If you take a closer look at the movement (Figure 10-5), you'll notice two intersecting rays: the arm and the forearm, meeting at the elbow. The area between them is called an **angle**. In Euclidean geometry, the arm and forearm are called **sides**, while the intersecting point is called **vertex**. To put it formally:

Euclidean angle is the figure between two rays (sides) sharing a common endpoint (vertex).

In our bicep curl example, the athlete is starting at an angle of about 170–180 degrees, with the forearm fully extended. The goal is to move the wrist above 90 degrees to complete the full range of motion.

Figure 10-5. *Left: the starting position of a bicep curl (~170 degrees). Right: the final position of a bice curl (~35 degrees)*

How do we measure the angle formed between three points in space? First, we need to properly identify the sides of the angle, a.k.a. the two segments (arm and forearm). In mathematics, we can represent each segment as a vector. A vector is nothing but a segment with direction. In our case:

- The arm vector has a direction from the elbow (point1) to the shoulder (point2).

- The forearm vector has a direction from the elbow (point1) to the wrist (point3).

- The angle between the vectors.

Since the elbow joint is the vertex of the angle, we are keeping it as the "starting point" of each vector. We'll use the Greek letter theta (θ) as a universal convention for naming an angle:

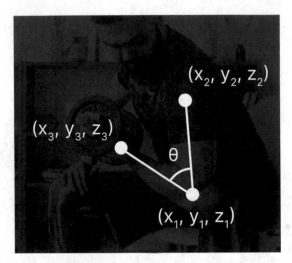

Figure 10-6. *Left: the starting position of a bicep curl (~170 degrees). Right: the final position of a bice curl (~35 degrees)*

Each vector has X, Y, and Z coordinates, calculated by subtracting the coordinates of the ending point from the starting point. In math terms:

$$a = \left(x_1 - x_2, y_1 - y_2, z_1 - z_2 \right)$$

$$b = \left(x_1 - x_3, y_1 - y_3, z_1 - z_3 \right)$$

And in C#:

```
Vector3 a = new Vector3(
    point1.X - point2.X,
    point1.Y - point2.Y,
    point1.Z - point2.Z);
Vector3 b = new Vector3(
    point1.X - point3.X,
    point1.Y - point3.Y,
    point1.Z - point3.Z);
```

We simplified the problem: the angle between three points is now the angle between two vectors. What's the formula for finding the angle? Trigonometry teaches us that "the dot product of two vectors is equal to the length of the first vector times the length of the second vector times the cosine of their angle." What does that mean in plain English? It's not our intention to go deep in trigonometry, so let's accept the preceding definition and break it down to its parts:

- The dot product of two vectors is a number produced by multiplying their respective coordinates.

- The length[5] of a vector is the distance between its two points (yea, we already did that in the previous section!)

- In a right triangle, the cosine of the angle is the number we get by dividing the length of the adjacent side by the length of the hypotenuse. **If we know the cosine, we know the angle!**

Here's the formula:

$$a{\cdot}b = |a||b|\cos \cos \theta$$

As a result, the cosine of the angle would be equal to

$$\cos \cos \theta = \frac{a{\cdot}b}{|a||b|}$$

Thankfully, math and computers have a function that returns the angle value given its cosine. That function is called inverse cosine (arcos). So the angle theta is equal to

$$\theta = arcos\theta \left(\frac{a{\cdot}b}{|a||b|} \right)$$

Trust me, the C# code is much clearer. Ready? First, we'll calculate the dot product of vectors a and b:

```
float dot = a.X * b.X + a.Y * b.Y + a.Z * b.Z;
```

---

[5] The length of a vector is commonly referred to as "magnitude."

Then, we'll calculate the length of each vector:

`float lengthA = Mathf.Sqrt(a.X * a.X + a.Y * a.Y + a.Z * a.Z);float`
`lengthB = Mathf.Sqrt(b.X * b.X + b.Y * b.Y + b.Z * b.Z);`

Last, we'll use the built-in Acos function to calculate the angle:

```
float theta = Mathf.Acos(dot / lengthA * lengthB);
```

Not so hard, right? There's one more thing to do: most of us are measuring angles in degrees. The official unit, however, is the radian. To convert the radians in degrees, we'll need to multiply the result by 180 and divide by the number π (pi).

```
theta *= 180.0f / Mathf.PI; // Radians to degrees
```

The number pi is a mathematical constant, approximately equal to 3.14. It represents the ratio of a circle's circumference to its diameter, which is always the same. You'll encounter that number a lot as your trigonometry skills advance.

If you are new to trigonometry but want to dive deeper and extend your skillset, I strongly recommend checking the web portal Math Open Reference.[6]

No more Greek – I promise! Now, just like we did for the `Distance()` method, we can extract a new method that measures the angle between three points. *To avoid* `DivideByZero` *exceptions, we are also going to check whether the lengths of the vectors are greater than zero.*

```
public float Angle(Vector3 point1, Vector3 point2, Vector3 point3)
{
    Vector3 a = new Vector3(
        point1.X - point2.X,
        point1.Y - point2.Y,
        point1.Z - point2.Z);

    Vector3 b = new Vector3(
        point1.X - point3.X,
        point1.Y - point3.Y,
```

```
        point1.Z - point3.Z);

    float dot = a.X * b.X + a.Y * b.Y + a.Z * b.Z;

    float lengthA = Mathf.Sqrt(a.X * a.X + a.Y * a.Y + a.Z * a.Z);
    float lengthB = Mathf.Sqrt(b.X * b.X + b.Y * b.Y + b.Z * b.Z);

    if (lengthA == 0.0f || lengthB == 0.0f)
    {
        return 0.0f;
    }

    float theta = Mathf.Acos(dot / lengthA * lengthB);

    theta *= 180.0f / Mathf.PI; // Radians to degrees

    return theta;
}
```

Finally, it's time to measure that bicep curl. Follow through.

Example: Counting Bicep Curls

We've done the hard work. All that remains is to use the method we created to measure the angle between the target joints:

```
Vector3 elbow =
    body.GetJoint(JointId.ElbowLeft).Position;
Vector3 shoulder =
    body.GetJoint(JointId.ShoulderLeft).Position;
Vector3 wrist =
    body.GetJoint(JointId.WristLeft).Position;

float angle = Angle(elbow, shoulder, wrist);

Debug.Log($"Bicep curl angle: {angle}");
```

At this point, I'm going to let you flex your muscles in front of your Kinect and see the results in real time. When you get back to the book, I'll show you how to count each curl.

Establishing a Threshold

Back? Good. As you are lifting the dumbbells, the angle ranges from about 180 degrees (lowest point) to about 30 degrees (highest point). And then again, for as many times as your body can endure. As fatigue starts, you are no longer able to move the dumbbell up and your forearms never get horizontal. To count a rep, we first need to identify a threshold: let's say that any angle lower than 70 degrees is fine – the rep counts. We'll create a new class named RepCounter, where we'll add the threshold constant, the repetition counter, and the Angle() method we created earlier.

```
public class RepCounter
{
    public const float Threshold = 70.0f;

    private int _counter = 0;

    public float Angle(Vector3 point1, Vector3 point2, Vector3 point3)
    {
        // Implementation as before...
    }

}
```

Increasing the Counter

What else would we need? To avoid counting the same repetition more than once, we'll keep track of the minimum angle, which is the highest point achieved (wrist going up). To determine if the wrist has started to go down, we'll also store the previous angle:

```
private float _min = float.MaxValue;
private float _previous = float.NaN;
```

The athlete should meet two requirements to increase the rep counter:

- The angle should be lower than the threshold value (wrist above horizontal).

- The previous angle should be lower than the current one (wrist starting to go down).

- The previous angle should be equal to the minimum angle (wrist reached maximum height).

I've named the method Check() and I'm passing the Skeleton object as a parameter. The method prints a message when the rep counter increases. Here is the preceding algorithm in C# code:

```csharp
public void Check(Skeleton body)
{
    Vector3 elbow =
        body.GetJoint(JointId.ElbowLeft).Position;
    Vector3 shoulder =
        body.GetJoint(JointId.ShoulderLeft).Position;
    Vector3 wrist =
        body.GetJoint(JointId.WristLeft).Position;

    float angle = Angle(elbow, shoulder, wrist);

    if (angle < _min)
    {
        _min = angle;
    }

    if (angle < Threshold)
    {
        if (_previous < angle && _previous == _min)
        {
            _counter++;

            Debug.Log($"Count: {_counter}");

            _min = float.MaxValue; // Reset
        }
    }

    _previous = angle;
}
```

In Unity3D, all you need to do is capture the Skeleton object and call Check() from inside the Update() method.

```csharp
public class Azure_Kinect_BicepCurls : MonoBehaviour
{
    [SerializeField] private KinectConfiguration _configuration;

    private readonly KinectSensor _kinect =
        new KinectSensor();

    private readonly RepCounter _bicepCurlCounter =
        new RepCounter();

    private void Start()
    {
        _kinect.Start(_configuration);
    }

    private void Update()
    {
        if (!_kinect.IsRunning) return;

        KinectData frame = _kinect.Update();

        if (frame != null && frame.Bodies.Count > 0)
        {
            Skeleton body = frame.Bodies[0];

            _bicepCurlCounter.Check(body);
        }
    }

    private void OnDestroy()
    {
        _kinect.Stop();
    }
}
```

There you have it! Your custom bicep curl counter is ready. Grab your dumbbells and let Kinect count your reps. Here's the complete RepCounter class for your reference:

```csharp
public class RepCounter
{
    public const float Threshold = 70.0f;

    private int _counter = 0;

    private float _min = float.MaxValue;
    private float _previous = float.NaN;

    public void Check(Skeleton body)
    {
        Vector3 elbow =
            body.GetJoint(JointId.ElbowLeft).Position;
        Vector3 shoulder =
            body.GetJoint(JointId.ShoulderLeft).Position;
        Vector3 wrist =
            body.GetJoint(JointId.WristLeft).Position;

        float angle = Angle(elbow, shoulder, wrist);

        if (angle < _min)
        {
            _min = angle;
        }

        if (angle < Threshold)
        {
            if (_previous < angle && _previous == _min)
            {
                _counter++;

                Debug.Log($"Count: {_counter}");

                _min = float.MaxValue; // Reset
            }
        }

        _previous = angle;
    }
```

```
public float Angle(Vector3 point1, Vector3 point2, Vector3 point3)
{
    Vector3 a = new Vector3(
        point1.X - point2.X,
        point1.Y - point2.Y,
        point1.Z - point2.Z);

    Vector3 b = new Vector3(
        point1.X - point3.X,
        point1.Y - point3.Y,
        point1.Z - point3.Z);

    float dot = a.X * b.X + a.Y * b.Y + a.Z * b.Z;

    float lengthA =
        Mathf.Sqrt(a.X * a.X + a.Y * a.Y + a.Z * a.Z);
    float lengthB =
        Mathf.Sqrt(b.X * b.X + b.Y * b.Y + b.Z * b.Z);

    if (lengthA == 0.0f || lengthB == 0.0f)
    {
        return 0.0f;
    }

    float theta = Mathf.Acos(dot / lengthA * lengthB);

    theta *= 180.0f / Mathf.PI; // Radians to degrees

    return theta;
}
}
```

As a (coding) exercise, use the algorithm to measure the reps of the right side too. Additionally, combine the knowledge you gained in this chapter to provide feedback regarding the following:

- The spine should remain straight during the movement.

- The ankles should be positioned hip wide.

- The knees should not bend more than 20 degrees.

Wait a minute. A complete body workout includes both weights and cardiovascular exercise. Cardio is considered essential because it increases your heart rate and allows for better overall health. There's no simpler form of cardio than walking, jogging, or sprinting. In the next pages, we are going to measure the speed of an athlete, passing in front of the camera.

Measuring Speed

Speed is how fast or slow an object is moving. Intuitively speaking, somebody is fast if she can travel a distance within a short time period. In physics, speed is defined as the rate at which a body travels some distance. As Galileo defined the formula:

$$v = \frac{d}{t}$$

Speed is measured in meters per second. In C#, the formula is straightforward:

```
float speed = distance / time;
```

Figure 10-7. *A person walking in and out of the field of view*

Thankfully, we already know how to measure distances using Kinect and C#. All we need to do is specify the proper time frames. Let's bring it all together.

Example: How Fast Are You Walking?

In order to measure a person's speed, we need to know the position of a standard joint in two timeframes. In the next sample project, we assume a person that's walking in front of the Kinect camera and another person is clicking two buttons: a start button and a stop button.

So we are going to create a SpeedMeasurement class with three methods: Start(), Stop(), and Check(). There we'll store the total distance traveled, as well as the two timestamps. Since we are grabbing Skeleton instances on a per-frame basis, we'll need to measure the distance between the current position and the previous position. Thus, the need to store the previous position of the person too. Of course, don't forget to add the Distance() utility method we implemented earlier.

```
public class SpeedMeasurement
{
    private float _distance = 0.0f;
    private Vector3 _previous = Vector3.Zero;

    private DateTime _startDate;
    private DateTime _endDate;

    public void Start()
    {
    }

    public void Stop()
    {
    }

    public void Check(Skeleton skeleton)
    {
    }

    public float Distance(Vector3 point1, Vector3 point2)
    {
        // Implementation omitted.
    }
}
```

The implementation of these methods is a piece of cake – we are simply building on top of the fundamentals we already mastered. As a reference joint, we'll use the Pelvis, which is closer to the person's center of mass. The Check() method would simply increase the distance traveled.

```
public void Check(Skeleton skeleton)
{
    Vector3 position =
        skeleton.GetJoint(JointId.Pelvis).Position;

    _distance += Distance(position, _previous);

    _previous = position;
}
```

The Start() method will initiate the process, and the Stop() method will measure how much time passed and then apply the formula and display the results.

```
public void Start()
{
    _startDate = DateTime.Now;
}

public void Stop()
{
    _endDate = DateTime.Now;

    float time = (float)(_endDate - _startDate).TotalSeconds;

    if (time > 0)
    {
        float speed = _distance / time;

        Debug.Log($"Speed is {speed} meters per second");
    }
}
```

You can now call the SpeedMeasurement methods in your MonoBehaviour class.

```csharp
public class Azure_Kinect_Speed : MonoBehaviour
{
    [SerializeField] private KinectConfiguration _configuration;

    private readonly KinectSensor _kinect = new KinectSensor();

    private readonly SpeedMeasurement _speedMeasurement = new
    SpeedMeasurement();

    private void Start()
    {
        _kinect.Start(_configuration);
    }

    private void Update()
    {
        if (!_kinect.IsRunning) return;

        KinectData frame = _kinect.Update();

        if (frame != null && frame.Bodies.Count > 0)
        {
            Skeleton body = frame.Bodies[0];

            _speedMeasurement.Check(body);
        }
    }

    private void OnDestroy()
    {
        _kinect.Stop();
    }

    // These should be event handlers for two Unity buttons.
    public void OnTimerStart()
    {
        _speedMeasurement.Start();
    }
```

```
    public void OnTimerStop()
    {
        _speedMeasurement.Stop();
    }
}
```

There you have it. You can now do some basic gait analysis on athletes or even help elderly people by evaluating their movement patterns. For your reference, here's the complete SpeedMeasurement class:

```
public class SpeedMeasurement
{
    private float _distance = 0.0f;
    private Vector3 _previous = Vector3.Zero;

    private DateTime _startDate;
    private DateTime _endDate;

    public void Start()
    {
        _startDate = DateTime.Now;
    }

    public void Stop()
    {
        _endDate = DateTime.Now;

        float time = (float)(_endDate - _startDate).TotalSeconds;

        if (time > 0)
        {
            float speed = _distance / time;

            Debug.Log($"Speed is {speed} meters per second");
        }
    }
```

```
public void Check(Skeleton skeleton)
{
    Vector3 position = skeleton.GetJoint(JointId.Pelvis).Position;

    _distance += Distance(position, _previous);

    _previous = position;
}

public float Distance(Vector3 point1, Vector3 point2)
{
    return Mathf.Sqrt(
        (point2.X - point1.X) * (point2.X - point1.X) +
        (point2.Y - point1.Y) *(point2.Y - point1.Y) +
        (point2.Z - point1.Z) *(point2.Z - point1.Z));
}
}
```

Key Points

In this chapter, we used Kinect to create a digital personal trainer and analyze the human motion in real time. We explored three types of measurements:

- Distances
- Angles
- Speed

We explored simple and intermediate scientific concepts, including Euclidean distances, Pythagorean angle calculations, and speed measurements in the 3D space. Overall, such advanced knowledge allows you to differentiate yourself from other developers and create breathtaking products that seem closer to magic.

PART IV

The "Azure" in Kinect

CHAPTER 11

Azure Cognitive Services

During these rapidly changing times,[1] one thing's for sure: Artificial Intelligence is rising. And it's growing fast. Robots may not take over the world anytime soon, but they can definitely help us create smarter digital solutions to solve a wide range of challenging problems. Unlike traditional software development, Artificial Intelligence focuses on scenarios that can't be tackled with purely algorithmic approaches.

Body tracking is one such example – it's impossible to develop an algorithmic solution that identifies human joints. After all, how would you decide whether a pixel corresponds to a nose, elbow, or knee? There is no straightforward solution, and that's why we delegated the problem to Artificial Intelligence in the first place. Of course, there are numerous similar scenarios, including

- Object detection

- Face recognition

- Optical character recognition

- Language translation

- Text to speech

- Voice recognition

- Anomaly detection

Wouldn't it be nice if we could have an easy way to integrate all that kind of functionality into our applications? Wouldn't it be a huge time saver if we could feed an AI system with data and get back information? Well, guess what?

---

[1] I am writing this book during the COVID-19 pandemic.

V. Pterneas, *Mastering the Microsoft Kinect*, https://doi.org/10.1007/978-1-4842-8070-6_11

There Is an API for That!

It turns out we can use a set of online services to interact with readily available Artificial Intelligence modules and pretrained Machine Learning models hosted online. That's possible, thanks to Azure.

But what exactly is Azure? Azure is Microsoft's flagship cloud computing platform. The Azure infrastructure allows developers to host and manage a plethora of services, including SQL databases, distributed systems, HTTP services, file storage, and more. Azure resides in data centers spread across the whole globe.

Figure 11-1. *The Microsoft Azure data centers across the globe, as of January 2021[2]*

Azure marked the start of an era where Microsoft shifted its business focus from monolithic Windows development to rich cloud services. The data centers you see in Figure 11-1 can host way smarter processes than dummy databases; they are home to the intelligent Azure Cognitive Services.

---

[2] Image credit: `http://microsoft.com`

Azure Cognitive Services

Azure Cognitive Services encapsulate standard processes related to Artificial Intelligence and Machine Learning problems. Cognitive Services expose APIs that allow you to call and perform specific tasks. You can think of them as black boxes, operating in three simple steps:

1. You specify the kind of service you would like to use (e.g., object detection or voice recognition).

2. You feed the service with input data (e.g., an image or audio file).

3. The service sends back the results (e.g., the objects' locations or the recognized text).

Microsoft provides a web portal where developers configure and deploy their Cognitive Services. Client applications can reach the desired services using plain-old HTTP requests. In this chapter, we'll see how to configure a service in a few easy steps. We'll then configure a Unity3D client application to consume the service, feed it with data, and display the results. For that purpose, we'll use the Azure SDK binaries right within Unity3D.

As a software developer, you don't need to be familiar with the AI or ML concepts. You can harness the full power of the Azure SDK using specific C# commands. Of course, if you are a seasoned Machine Learning scientist, you can use Azure to train custom Machine Learning models. In this book, we'll focus on what is already available and supported by Microsoft Azure.

Before exploring the world of Cognitive Services, it's essential to clarify how the Azure approach differs from what we have been doing so far.

Offline Approach

So far, we have been interacting with the Machine Learning model offline: the ONNX neural network file was loaded directly into our application folder. Every time we distribute a Kinect body-tracking application, we need to distribute the 160MB model file too. Here is what's happening under the hood:

- The input device captures the required input data (image, voice, text, etc.).

- The application feeds the image to a local neural network.

- The neural network produces some output.

- The application uses the output.

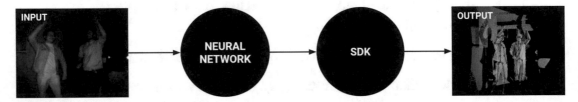

Figure 11-2. *Using a neural network offline*

Online Approach

Imagine if the model file is residing on a remote server, instead. You wouldn't need to package it into your application. You would only need an HTTP API to access it over the network. Moreover, you could update the Machine Learning model without making any changes to the client application! This way, your apps become automatically smarter without you having to release a software update package. In an online approach, this is how the interaction changes when the cloud is involved:

- The input device captures the required input data (image, voice, text, etc.).

- The application transmits the input to Azure.

- An Azure Cognitive Service feeds the input to the neural network.

- The neural network produces some output.

- The output is transmitted over the network back to the application.

- The application uses the output.

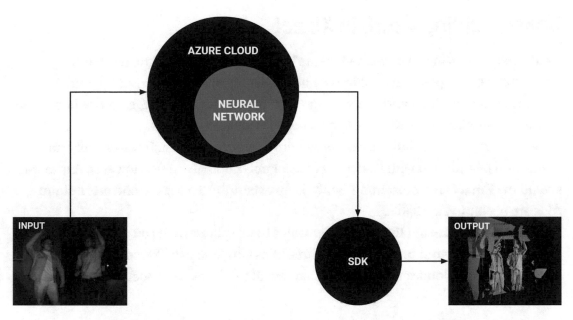

Figure 11-3. *Using a neural network online, over the Azure cloud*

As you understand, running a network online has the overhead of the Internet connection. Data needs to travel over the Internet to reach the cloud and then again to get back to your computer. As a result, the experience may not be real time. Body tracking is considered a heavy operation, so there would be substantial wait times if we were to run such a body-tracking neural network over the Internet.

Hopefully, as wireless connectivity technology is evolving to provide faster speeds,[3] we'll be able to run neural networks solely over the web. For now, we'll focus on lighter neural networks, such as Microsoft's object detection.

What about a hybrid approach? Many fellow developers and coworkers ask whether we could combine the best of both worlds – meaning a Machine Learning model running on the cloud and a local model when the network is not available. As of now, this possibility is not supported by the Azure Cognitive Services, but it's an open field for you to experiment with.

---

[3] I'm looking at you, 5G.

Understanding Azure in Kinect

As it's clear now, Kinect was named "Azure" as part of Microsoft's greater vision for Artificial Intelligence. Everything is interconnected around Microsoft's cloud infrastructure: Windows and Office integrate with OneDrive, a storage service hosted on Azure. In a similar sense, Kinect integrates with Cognitive Services.

At its core, though, Kinect does not require an Azure account. It can entirely run offline and provide you with its rich set of color and depth features. However, Azure can extend the Kinect and, most importantly, keep expanding it as more and more cloud APIs are becoming available.

However, you are not limited to Microsoft's Azure platform. If you decide to use a cloud provider for your projects, you are free to use anyone you like, such as Amazon's AWS or Google's Cloud services. In the chapters of this book, we'll focus on Azure for three reasons:[4]

- Cognitive Services provide a diverse collection of Machine Learning models, suitable for a variety of use-case scenarios.

- Azure comes with easy-to-use tools and software development kits to connect to the server with minimum effort.

- It's free to use for rapid prototyping, making it an affordable solution to try out immediately.

Creating a Computer Vision API

Since you have a good understanding of the approach, let's connect to an Azure account and create a Cognitive Service. First, you need a Microsoft Azure account, so if you don't already have one, go to `https://portal.azure.com/` and create one. Otherwise, log in to your existing account.

---

[4] Disclaimer: I am not paid by Microsoft to advertise its cloud platform. Neither am I an affiliate of Azure. I have been developing Azure applications for the past eight years. Recommending Azure is just my personal preference and opinion.

A note on price: As of the day of this writing, creating an Azure account is free of charge. Some Azure services are also free of charge so that you can experiment without any risk. Upon exceeding the free credit limit, Microsoft will charge you based on the resource consumption and storage volume you are using. Learn more in the official Azure Pricing Calculator: `https://azure.microsoft.com/en-us/pricing/calculator/`

So log in to your Azure account and visit the Azure Portal. Its homepage demonstrates shortcuts to a few commonly used Azure services. Don't forget that Azure is mainly a cloud hosting provider, so don't be discouraged by the overwhelming amount of information related to database and storage services.

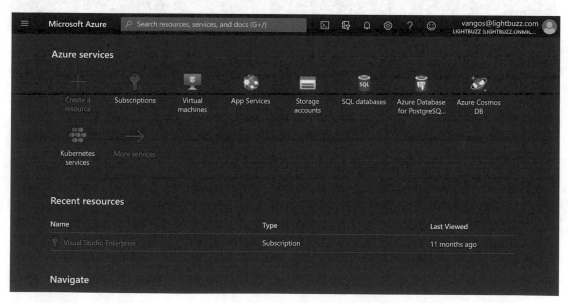

Figure 11-4. *The Microsoft Azure Portal home page*

To find the Artificial Intelligence APIs, you need to click the Menu icon and visit the Dashboard, as shown in Figure 11-5.

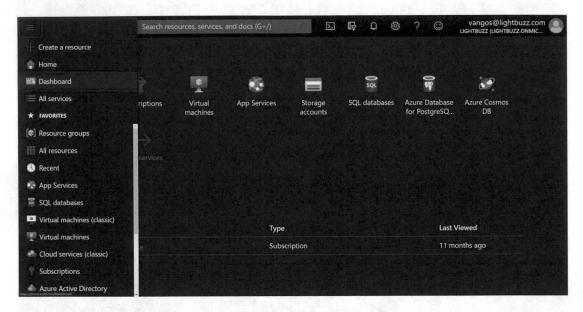

Figure 11-5. *The Azure Portal menu and Dashboard link*

The Dashboard includes a list of everyday actions. Cognitive Services are not parts of the standard functionality; they are add-ons. You can think of add-ons like packaged components that extend the Azure cloud functionality. In our case, we'll extend Azure with Computer Vision services. All such add-ons can be found in the Azure **Marketplace**, a curated database of various such components. So click the Marketplace button from your Dashboard.

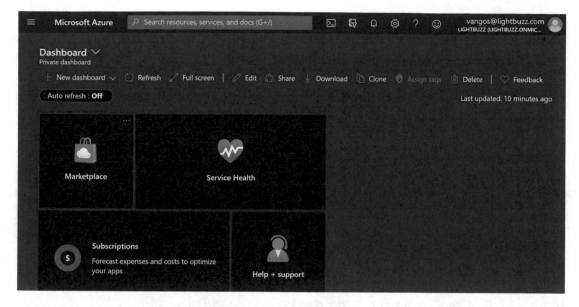

Figure 11-6. *The Azure Dashboard*

As you can see in Figure 11-7, the Marketplace is organized into multiple sections, such as Databases, Analytics, and Blockchain. For our purpose, select the **AI + Machine Learning** category. You'll see a list of AI- and ML-related add-ons from various providers. Scroll until you find the service named **Computer Vision**, published by Microsoft.

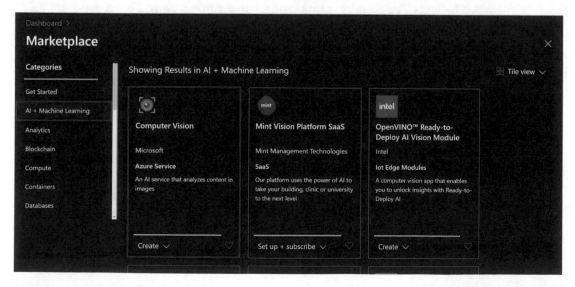

Figure 11-7. *The Azure Marketplace, searching for Computer Vision services*

You should see some descriptive information about what you are going to install. Things are getting exciting! Go on and click the **Create** button to add a new Computer Vision service to your Azure plan.

Figure 11-8. *Creating a new Computer Vision Cognitive Service*

The next screen prompts you to configure the new service. You need to fill in the details before moving forward carefully. At this point, especially if you've never worked with Azure in the past, it's natural to feel overwhelmed by the amount of information you need to provide. Trust me; it's pretty straightforward. Here is precisely what you need to type to each option:

- Subscription – That's your Azure cloud subscription plan. Leave the default option if you've just created an Azure account.

- Resource group – Resource groups are containers for Azure resources. A resource group usually includes related modules and add-ons. Unless you have an existing Computer Vision project, I recommend you to create a new resource group. Give it a descriptive name so you can easily access or delete it in the future.

- Region – That's the deployment location of the new service. Azure has data centers across the world. Select an area that's closer to where your company is.

- Name – The name of the new Cognitive Service. I've used the term "KinectCognitiveService" for my demos.

- Pricing tier – Be careful here. There are two pricing tiers with different features each. The more you use the service, the more calls you'll make and the more resources you'll use (and, consequently, the higher the price you'll pay). However, the free tier allows up to 20 calls per minute, which makes it ideal for testing purposes.[5] I suggest you start with the Free tier and move to a paid one when in production.

Figure 11-9 shows my configuration for the service. Feel free to copy it for your "hello world" projects.

Figure 11-9. *Specifying the Computer Vision service details (name, pricing, region, etc.)*

---

[5] In case you exceed the amounts of API calls you can make, the service will throw a timeout exception.

After you've specified the desired configuration, click the **Review + create** button and wait a few seconds for Azure to perform a quick validation (Figure 11-10).

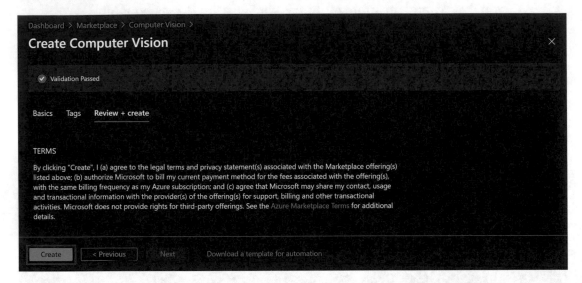

Figure 11-10. *Successful creation of a new Computer Vision service*

When the validation is passed, click **Create** to see your new service (Figure 11-11). No need to do any further actions.

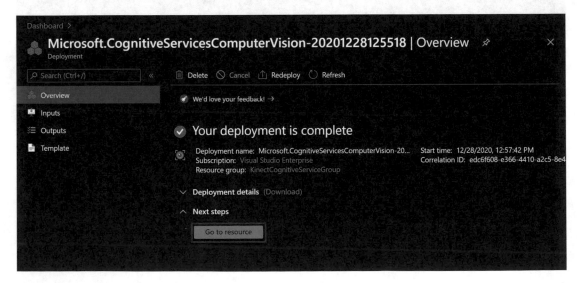

Figure 11-11. *Overview of the Computer Vision service*

Our Computer Vision service is ready! Click **Go to resource** to see the accessibility details. Our service exists somewhere in the cloud. How are we going to access it? Thankfully, Microsoft has already created a REST API under the hood for us. No need to perform additional server configuration. All we need is a way to access this REST API. Go to the **Keys and Endpoint** section of the service.

The **Key 1** and **Endpoint** parameters are all we need to access the service. The Endpoint specifies the location of the service on the World Wide Web. The Key value is a unique alphanumeric sequence that allows your applications to access the service. When calling the service, Azure will authenticate you based on the provided key. After all, you don't want someone else to access your service and exploit your resources, right?

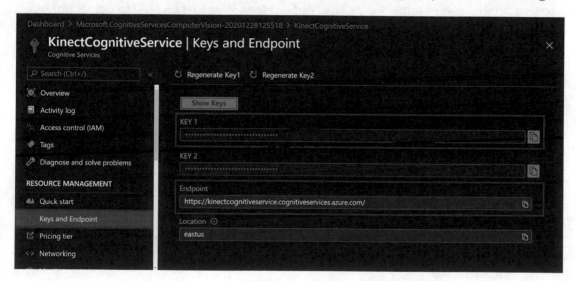

Figure 11-12. *The API keys and Endpoint of the Computer Vision service*

Copy the Key 1 and Endpoint parameters to a secure location as we'll need for the upcoming chapters.

Key Points

In this chapter, we finally understood why Kinect has "Azure" in its name. We extended our AI reach to the cloud by creating an online Computer Vision service. Online Artificial Intelligence APIs act as an intermediate layer: they accept a specific input and provide the corresponding output. Instead of using the resources of our local computers, they are delegating the heavy neural network tasks to a remote server. That is greatly extending our options and allows developers to create smarter applications without worrying about the hardware.

We have only scratched the surface of what's possible with the Azure Cognitive Services. In the next chapter, we will use the service we've just created to detect objects within the Kinect's field of view.

A Demo Service for You

In case you would like to experiment with Azure but would not want to create an account, feel free to use the credentials of a demo account I created for this book. This way, you can try the Computer Vision services right away. Use with care, and remember to create your own account before releasing your app to production.

- Key: 7946df2b7faa47e18d61f5245b18e334

- Endpoint: `https://kinectcognitiveservice.cognitiveservices.azure.com/`

CHAPTER 12

Computer Vision and Object Detection

In the previous chapter, we created a cloud API to make our applications even smarter. With only a few keystrokes, we created an Azure Cognitive Service capable of performing Computer Vision tasks. So far, the service is doing nothing but patiently residing on the cloud and expecting us to call it. Moving forward, we will feed Microsoft's AI with Kinect's color data to detect a variety of objects. Such objects include cars, people, televisions, phones, laptops, dogs, cats, and even teddy bears. We won't stop there, though. Then, using the Kinect's depth data, we'll measure the distance between each object and the camera! Here's an overview of the process:

1. Capture the Kinect color and depth frames.

2. Feed the RGB color data to the Azure Computer Vision service.

3. Let Azure process the data.

4. Retrieve the coordinates of the detected objects.

5. Use the depth frame to measure the distance of each object.

© Vangos Pterneas 2022
V. Pterneas, *Mastering the Microsoft Kinect*, https://doi.org/10.1007/978-1-4842-8070-6_12

Figure 12-1 shows the raw Kinect data before sending them to the cloud.

Figure 12-1. *The synchronized Kinect color and depth frames*

Figure 12-2 shows what the end result is going to look like upon processing.

Figure 12-2. *The object-detection and depth measurement results*

As you understand, to follow along with this chapter, you need to have an understanding of the Azure Cognitive Services (Chapter 11), Kinect color (Chapter 4), and depth (Chapter 5) data, as well as coordinate mapping (Chapter 9). In case you are not familiar with these concepts, get back to the corresponding chapters to refresh your knowledge. I'll wait.

Done? Good. Let's do some more AI magic.

Do You Need a Kinect After All?

The Azure Cognitive Services can accept any type of image as input. All they need is a binary representation of the desired picture, nothing more. Cognitive Services are device agnostic, and as such, they are not tied to a particular camera.

For the first parts of the process, you do not need a Kinect device to detect objects in live video streams. Figure 12-3 shows the result of computer vision processing on a traditional RGB photo. So most video cameras would do the job just fine, and you can use your knowledge across a variety of input sources.

Figure 12-3. *Azure Cognitive Services are not limited to the Kinect. This picture has applied the same object-detection process on a photo captured with a typical camera[1]*

However, you need a Kinect device to estimate the distance between the detected objects and the camera and make your apps stand out. That's precisely where depth cameras come in handy. The Cognitive Service API will only give you the coordinates of each object's bounding box. In the preceding photo, you would know that a person is on

---

[1] Photo by Jeremy Bishop on Unsplash.

the left, while a car is on the right. Using the depth data information, you also know that the person has a 2-meter distance from the car and 3 meters from our perspective. Now, that's a totally new world of opportunities!

Let's find out how we can add this kind of functionality to our existing Kinect application.

The Azure Cognitive Services SDK

Cognitive Services are HTTP web services we can access using their respective REST APIs. REST is a web protocol that allows client applications to exchange information with servers. A REST HTTP request is a command sent by an app to a server that specifies what kind of information it needs. The request is formatted as a traditional URL. You can think of this process as a communication mechanism between remote computers. For example, a client application may send a command to fetch some data, and the server will respond by providing the requested information. The available commands are called endpoints. Any application that can make web requests can access and interact with those endpoints.

The Computer Vision Cognitive Service defines its own endpoints. If you are interested in diving deeper into this technology, Microsoft has well documented the API calls and provides open source samples on GitHub.[2]

Up to this point, you may assume that we are going to write web-related code to access the API – and that wouldn't be fun at all, right? Thankfully for us, the official Azure SDKs provide a level of abstraction, so we don't need to write the web-related methods from scratch. Instead of directly implementing HTTP requests, we will use the C# wrappers and let the SDK do the heavy lifting for us. Similar to what we did in Chapter 2 with the Machine Learning part, we'll add the proper binaries into our Unity project and use the appropriate APIs to interact with the remote service.

---

[2] https://github.com/Azure-Samples/cognitive-services-REST-api-samples

The Computer Vision NuGet Package

Microsoft is distributing most of its Azure packages via NuGet, a platform for sharing and managing third-party .NET libraries. To install the Computer Vision package, launch Unity3D and select *Assets* ➤ *Open C# project* to launch Visual Studio.

In Visual Studio, select *Tools* ➤ *NuGet Package Manager* ➤ *Manage NuGet Packages for Solution*. This should open the NuGet Package Manager window, where you can search for packages. In the search box, type the name of the package we need, which is

`Microsoft.Azure.CognitiveServices.Vision.ComputerVision`

NuGet should display the official Microsoft Computer Vision package on top of the search results, as in Figure 12-4. Click the package and check the Assembly-CSharp option. This option specifies the target project we would like to install the package in. Lastly, click the *Install* button to download the binaries.

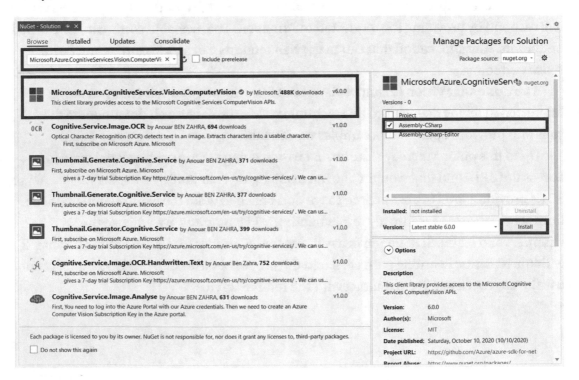

Figure 12-4. *The Azure Computer Vision NuGet package*

After you click Install, you'll be prompted to accept the software license agreement. Proceed and wait a few seconds for the package to install.

Attention   Unlike native Visual Studio projects, installing a NuGet package in a Unity3D project will not make that package visible by Unity, and our project is not yet able to detect the binaries. We need to configure it manually.

By default, the package contents are located in the *Packages* folder of our Unity project, right next to the Assets folder. Go on and open the Packages folder to reveal its contents, as in Figure 12-5.

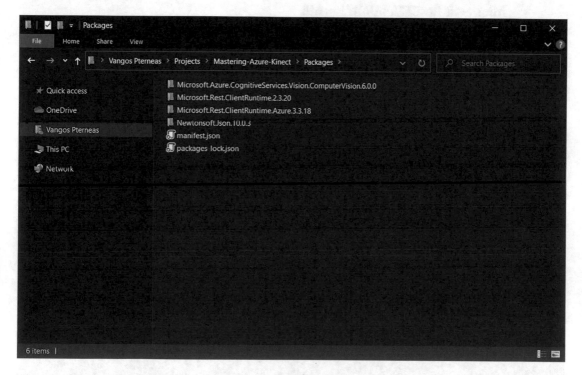

Figure 12-5. *The installed Computer Vision NuGet packages*

Importing the Packages in Unity3D

The Packages include the binaries we need, but Unity can't see them yet. We need to import the DLL files to the *Plugins* Editor folder. Launch the Unity Kinect project and expand the Plugins directory. Then, go back to the Packages, and open the following subfolders, which include the necessary binaries:

- Packages\Microsoft.Azure.CognitiveServices.Vision. ComputerVision.6.0.0\lib\net461

- Packages\Microsoft.Rest.ClientRuntime.2.3.20\lib\net461

- Packages\Microsoft.Rest.ClientRuntime.Azure.3.3.18\lib\net452

- Packages\Newtonsoft.Json.10.0.3\lib\net45

In the end, you should copy (or drag and drop) the following four binaries in your Plugins, right next to Azure Kinect Sensor binaries:

- Microsoft.Azure.CognitiveServices.Vision.ComputerVision.dll

- Microsoft.Rest.ClientRuntime.dll

- Microsoft.Rest.ClientRuntime.Azure.dll

- Newtonsoft.Json.dll

The updated Unity project structure should look like Figure 12-6.

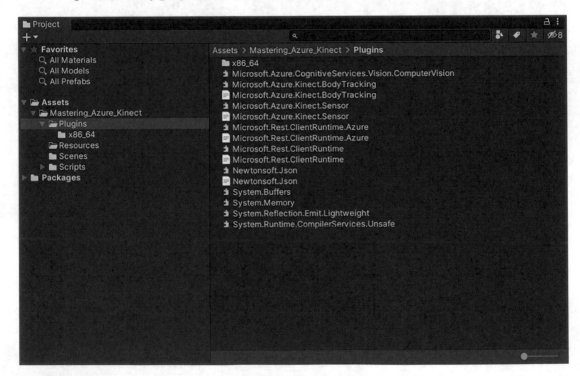

Figure 12-6. *The new Azure Computer Vision binaries inside Unity's Plugins folder*

In my setup, I have also added the corresponding XML documentation files, along with the DLLs. This way, Visual Studio's IntelliSense will display the documentation tooltip whenever we use the newly added classes.

Creating a New Unity Scene

Now, Unity can properly detect and compile the Azure Computer Vision binaries. We have successfully integrated yet another SDK, so let's go on and create a new Unity scene to test it. Building on top of what we have already learned, start by making a clone of the Color scene we created in Chapter 4. I named the new script **Azure_Kinect_ComputerVision.cs**. Remember to include a RawImage component, as well as the configuration script to control the device.

In the Editor, the new scene would look like Figure 12-7.

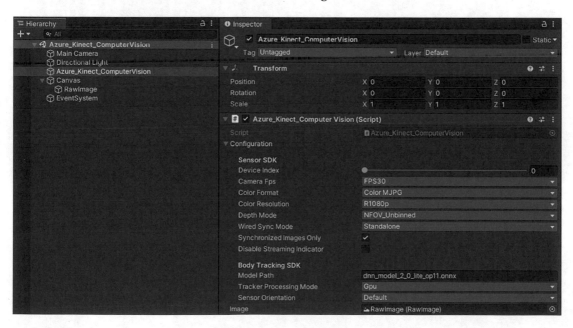

Figure 12-7. *The new Unity scene for Azure Computer Vision*

The bare-bones code of that scene is straightforward:

```
using System.IO;
using UnityEngine;
using UnityEngine.UI;
```

```
public class Azure_Kinect_ComputerVision : MonoBehaviour
{
    [SerializeField] private KinectConfiguration _configuration;
    [SerializeField] private RawImage _image;

    private readonly KinectSensor _kinect = new KinectSensor();

    private Texture2D _texture;

    private void Start()
    {
        _kinect.Start(_configuration);

        _texture = new Texture2D(1, 1, TextureFormat.RGB24, false);
        _image.texture = _texture;
    }

    private void Update()
    {
        if (!_kinect.IsRunning) return;

        KinectData frameData = _kinect.Update();
    }

    private void OnDestroy()
    {
        _kinect.Stop();
    }
}
```

In the configuration settings, remember to leave the Color Format option to MJPEG. You'll see why in a while.

Referencing the Azure Computer Vision SDK

The code is controlling the Kinect device and displays the color data. To add Azure interactivity, we need to import the new Azure namespaces:

```
using Microsoft.Azure.CognitiveServices.Vision.ComputerVision;
using Microsoft.Azure.CognitiveServices.Vision.ComputerVision.Models;
```

We can now access the Azure SDK classes. Remember the API key and endpoint we created in the previous chapter? It's time to use these values. In C#, create two constants and paste the values you copied from the Azure Portal. In the following example, I've copied my own key and endpoint:

```
private const string VisionApiKey = "8991690980884ab6b2a8188c542a77c7";
private const string VisionEndpoint = "https://lightbuzzcomputervision.
cognitiveservices.azure.com/";
```

I can almost hear you asking how are we going to use these values? Meet ComputerVisionClient, a C# class that allows us to connect to our Azure Computer Vision service, feed it with data, and fetch the object detection results. The ComputerVisionClient needs the key and endpoint parameters in order to connect. So let's create and initialize it:

```
private readonly ComputerVisionClient _azure =
    new ComputerVisionClient(new
        ApiKeyServiceClientCredentials(VisionApiKey))
        {
            Endpoint = VisionEndpoint
        };
```

The _azure object is our interface with Azure in the same way the _kinect object is our interface with Kinect. Let's explore how we can use it.

Computer Vision in Action

The Computer Vision client we just referenced has a very simple and straightforward API. We created it by providing our unique key and endpoint. These two parameters guarantee that our app will communicate with our own Azure service and nothing else. The Computer Vision client has only one job: detect objects in streams of images. The job is accomplished by calling the method DetectObjectsInStreamAsync.

Input: Kinect Color Frames

The DetectObjectsInStreamAsync method needs a JPEG-encoded stream as its input. That's exactly why I told you to use the MJPEG color format in the Kinect configuration! Kinect is serving its color frames to the format required by Azure. We already know how to acquire the color data in the Update() method:

```
byte[] colorData = frameData.Color;
```

Converting the JPEG array to a C# stream is also straightforward:

```
using (Stream stream = new MemoryStream(colorData))
{
    // Use the stream here...
}
```

As you noticed, we enclosed the stream into a using statement. The using statement guarantees that the stream will dispose of any unmanaged resources when it exits the block. Now, we can call the object detection method:

```
DetectResult result =
    await _azure.DetectObjectsInStreamAsync(stream);
```

Under the hood, the method is encapsulating a ton of functionality, and as a result, it's running asynchronously. The Computer Vision client is creating the HTTP request, authenticating with Azure, and waiting for the detection results. Such tasks take time. Asynchronous methods execute long-running operations on a separate thread without blocking our main thread. Since we are using the await keyword, we would better extract an async method:[3]

```
private async void DetectObjects(byte[] colorData)
{
    using (Stream stream = new MemoryStream(colorData))
```

---

[3] In case you are not familiar with asynchronous C# programming, consider reading Microsoft's Getting Started guides: https://docs.microsoft.com/en-us/dotnet/csharp/programming-guide/concepts/async/

```
    {
        DetectResult result =
            await _azure.DetectObjectsInStreamAsync(stream);
    }
}
```

Experienced web developers would notice two issues with the preceding code:

- There are no safety nets if the web requests fail, for example, due to lack of an Internet connection.

- Since the method runs asynchronously, and Kinect is serving 30 frames per second, it may be accidentally executed multiple times per second before completion.

The first objection may be rare, but it's valid, and we need to account for it. There are numerous scenarios where a web request could fail. For example, the computer may lose connectivity to the Internet, or the Azure service may be accidentally deleted. In such cases, the web request would fail, and the application will not continue execution. As responsible developers, we'll handle such occasions by wrapping the web request into a try-catch block.

```
private async void DetectObjects(byte[] colorData)
{
    try
    {
        using (Stream stream = new MemoryStream(colorData))
        {
            DetectResult result = await _azure.DetectObjectsInStreamAsync
            (stream);
        }
    }
    catch
    {
        // Provide a message to the user.
    }
}
```

The second point is easier to miss, especially if you are not familiar with multithreaded code execution. Kinect is streaming 30 frames per second. Web requests are time-consuming operations, so chances are we won't be able to send 30 web requests and receive 30 responses every second – it's inevitable to analyze fewer frames than we stream. What would happen if the main thread tries to access the asynchronous operation before it's completed? You guessed right: a runtime exception. We need to ensure that no other thread will interact with the Azure client while Azure is processing data. The simplest way to achieve this is by using a Boolean flag:

```
private bool _isProcessing = false;

private async void DetectObjects(byte[] colorData)
{
    if (_isProcessing) return;

    try
    {
        _isProcessing = true;

        using (Stream stream = new MemoryStream(colorData))
        {
            DetectResult result = await _azure.DetectObjectsInStreamAsync
            (stream);
        }

        _isProcessing = false;
    }
    catch
    {
        // Provide a message to the user.
    }
}
```

The Boolean member _isProcessing becomes true when we start the request and false when the request is finished. In case another thread tries to access the Azure client while it's running, the flag will simply prevent it from reaching the critical statements. The request is fully protected! All we need is call the DetectObjects() method from the Update() method:

```csharp
private void Update()
{
    if (!_kinect.IsRunning) return;

    KinectData frameData = _kinect.Update();

    if (frameData != null)
    {
        byte[] colorData = frameData.Color;

        _texture.LoadImage(colorData);

        DetectObjects(colorData);
    }
}
```

Hardcore developers may create additional Azure clients and synchronize their responses, thus resulting in higher frame rates. However, that would be an advanced topic not covered by this book.

Output: Object Rectangles

When the web request safely returns, it has packaged the results in the form of a DataResult object. The DataResult class includes the Objects property, which, you guessed, provides all the information we need about the detected objects. We can loop into the Objects list and explore its contents:

```csharp
foreach (DetectedObject item in result.Objects)
{
    Debug.Log($"Type: {item.ObjectProperty}");
    Debug.Log($"Confidence: {item.Confidence}");
    Debug.Log($"Position: {item.Rectangle.X}, {item.Rectangle.Y}");
    Debug.Log($"Size: {item.Rectangle.W}x{item.Rectangle.H}");
}
```

Each item of the array is an instance of the `DetectedObject` class. Detected objects include the following properties:

- ObjectProperty – The name of the item, for example, "computer," "phone," "dog," "cat," "keyboard," "car," etc.

- Confidence – A number between 0.0 and 1.0, indicating the tracking confidence of the object or how sure AI is about that particular object

- Rectangle – The position of the top-left corner of the object's area (X &Y), as well as the width (W) and height (H) of the rectangle

---

There's also one extra property called **Parent**. The Parent member is another DetectedObject that specifies whether the object is enclosed into another one. For example, if Azure sees a "person" inside a "car," the "car" would be the parent object of the "person." That feature allows you to make sense of the objects' relations and provide your customers with a richer experience.

Let's get to the fun part now. Run the code, point Kinect to some objects, and check what's the output in the Unity console window! In my case, it looks like this:

```
Type: keyboard
Confidence: 0.631
Position: 197, 605
Size: 537x271

Type: person
Confidence: 0.905
Position: 571, 135
Size: 612x801
```

That's right, Kinect is looking at a person (me) holding a keyboard!

Coordinate Mapping

So far, we have been able to detect objects within a color frame and print their characteristics. Time to use the power of Kinect and take it a step forward. Our application will become smarter by knowing the distance between each object and the camera.

As we've learned in Chapter 9, the Kinect SDK can transform between the 2D and the 3D space. In our case, we know the position of the rectangular area of the objects within the RGB color frame. The rectangle is described by the coordinates of the top-left corner, as well as its width and height. The center of the object would be the center of its bounding rectangle, as shown in Figure 12-8.

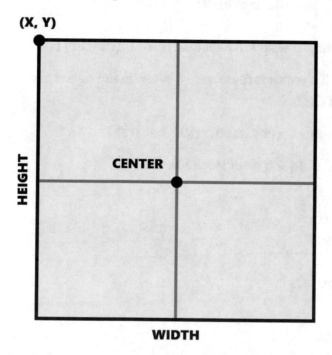

Figure 12-8. *The center of a bounding rectangle, in relation to the top-left corner, width, and height*

We have enough information to estimate the coordinates (X and Y) of the center of the rectangle by applying some dead simple maths:

```
foreach (DetectedObject item in result.Objects)
{
    BoundingRect rect = item.Rectangle;

    int centerX = rect.X + rect.W / 2;
    int centerY = rect.Y + rect.H / 2;
}
```

Given the center of the object in the 2D color space, we can now use Kinect's coordinate mapping functions to get its position in the 3D world space. We have already implemented such a method in the KinectSensor class back in Chapter 9.

```
Vector2 center =
    new Vector2(centerX, centerY);
Vector3 position =
    _kinect.CoordinateMapper.MapColorToWorld(center);
```

The z value of the vector is the distance between the object and the camera. We can print the numbers like before:

```
Debug.Log($"Distance: {position.z:N2} meters");
```

So the updated Unity log would look like this:

```
Type: keyboard
Confidence: 0.631
Position: 197, 605
Size: 537x271
Distance: 0.72 meters

Type: person
Confidence: 0.905
Position: 571, 135
Size: 612x801
Distance: 0.84 meters
```

Visualizing the Results

Console output is useful, but we can do much better in terms of user interface design. Instead of printing the values, let's draw some rectangles around the detected objects, which would definitely be more intuitive. Our code will generate one rectangle per object, positioned at the proper location. Each rectangle will also feature two labels – one to display the object title and another to display its distance from the camera.

As a first step, I created a couple of Unity UI elements in my Editor's Hierarchy view. The elements include

- An Image container that will be acting as the border of the rectangle

- A text field at the top of the image to display the object type

- A second text field at the bottom of the image to display the distance value

I've named the container with the descriptive title **Detected Object Rectangle** and extracted it as a prefab in my Resources folder. To create a prefab in Unity, all you need to do is drag and drop the UI container into the Project's Resources folder.

To update the position, size, and text values of my new prefab, I created a script named **DetectedObjectRectangle.cs** and attached it to the prefab. The script contains references to the three UI elements:

```
public class DetectedObjectRectangle : MonoBehaviour
{
    [SerializeField] private Image _border;
    [SerializeField] private Text _textType;
    [SerializeField] private Text _textDistance;
}
```

Of course, to properly reference the elements, we need to drag and drop them from the Hierarchy to their corresponding Inspector fields, as shown in Figure 12-9.

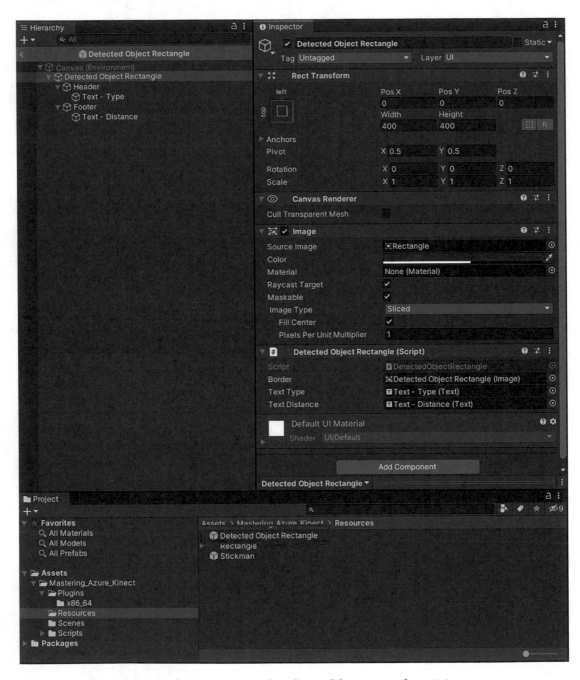

Figure 12-9. *A rectangle element with adjustable size and position*

The component does not do anything yet. Let's implement a method that will update its state. What do we need to know to correctly position and display the visual element?

- The title of the object (string)

- The center of the object (X and Y – Vector2)

- The size of the object (width and height – Vector2).

- The Z distance from the camera (float) or the position in the 3D space (Vector3)

I've created a method named Load() and added those values as parameters. Load() is updating the user interface according to the specified values:

```
public void Load(string type, Vector2 center, Vector2 size, Vector3
position)
{
    // The title of the object.
    _textType.text = type;

    // The distance from the camera (Z value of the XYZ position vector).
    _textDistance.text = position.z.ToString("N2") + "m";

    // The 2D position of the center of the element.
    _border.rectTransform.anchoredPosition = new Vector2(center.x,
    -center.y);

    // The size of the rectangle.
    _border.rectTransform.sizeDelta = size;
}
```

Back to the main scene, our application will need to create one rectangle component for every object detected. Since we don't know how many objects the service will recognize, we'll dynamically generate the proper number of rectangle components. As a result, we need to add a reference to the prefab element into the application scene (in my case, **Azure_Kinect_ComputerVision.cs**).

```
[SerializeField] private GameObject _detectedObjectPrefab;
```

Since we are using a Canvas-based Unity UI, we'll reference the Canvas as the parent element of the prefabs.

```
[SerializeField] private Transform _canvas;
```

253

Figure 12-10 shows the properly referenced prefab and canvas.

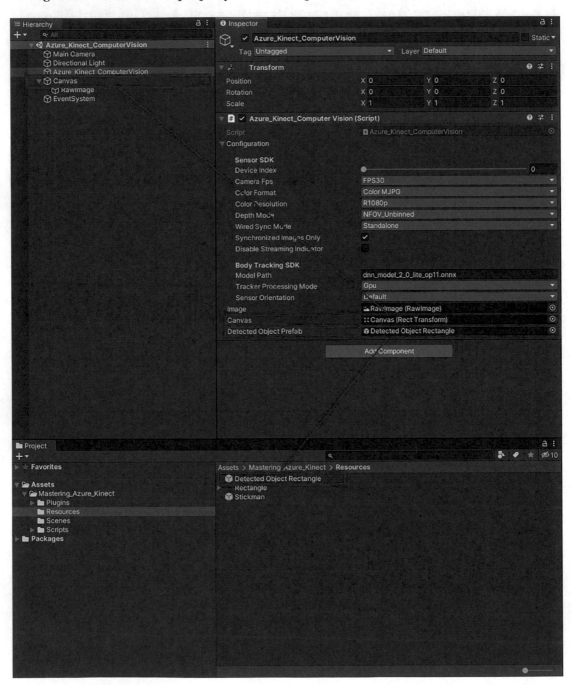

Figure 12-10. *Referencing the prefab and canvas objects in the Unity Editor*

We'll use a C# List collection to hold the generated rectangles:

```
private readonly List<DetectedObjectRectangle> _rectangles = new List<Detec
tedObjectRectangle>();
```

When Azure returns the detected objects, our app should generate the proper number of rectangles. In case the size of the collection is equal to the size of the objects, we'll keep the rectangles as is and only update their values. Otherwise, we have to re-generate the collection to match the new number of objects. We'll use the Clear() method to remove the elements from the List and the Destroy() method to delete any existing rectangles from the user interface.

```
DetectResult result = await _azure.DetectObjectsInStreamAsync(stream);

if (result.Objects.Count != _rectangles.Count)
{
    foreach (DetectedObjectRectangle rectangle in _rectangles)
    {
        Destroy(rectangle.gameObject);
    }

    _rectangles.Clear();
}
```

After clearing the existing items, we'll generate the new ones by instantiating the prefab referenced in our main scene. Remember to use the Canvas reference as their parent. The newly created element will be added to the List:

```
foreach (DetectedObject item in result.Objects)
{
    GameObject go = Instantiate(_detectedObjectPrefab, _canvas);
    DetectedObjectRectangle rectangle = go.GetComponent<DetectedObject
    Rectangle>();

    _rectangles.Add(rectangle);
}
```

The last part is relatively easy. Wherever we used Debug.Log() to print the values, we'll instead call the Load() method to update the visual elements.

```
for (int i = 0; i < result.Objects.Count; i++)
{
    DetectedObject item = result.Objects[i];
    DetectedObjectRectangle rectangle = _rectangles[i];

    BoundingRect rect = item.Rectangle;

    int centerX = rect.X + rect.W / 2;
    int centerY = rect.Y + rect.H / 2;

    string title = item.ObjectProperty;
    Vector2 center = new Vector2(centerX, centerY);
    Vector2 size = new Vector2(rect.W, rect.H);
    Vector3 position = _kinect.CoordinateMapper.MapColorToWorld(center);

    rectangle.Load(title, center, size, position);
}
```

And there you have it! Run the project, and you'll see the results of Figure 12-2 in action. You can download the source code from the repository of this book.

Closing the Service

If you reached this point, congratulations! You have effectively combined the power of the Kinect camera with the possibilities of the Azure Computer Vision services. It's easy to miss, but there's one extra step we need to do before closing the application: the service needs to dispose of unmanaged resources, so we have to call the Dispose() method when we no longer need the service. In our case, we'll add it in the OnDestroy() method, right after we shut down the Kinect device:

```
private void OnDestroy()
{
    _kinect.Stop();
    _azure.Dispose();

    foreach (DetectedObjectRectangle rectangle in _rectangles)
    {
        if (rectangle.isActiveAndEnabled)
```

```
    {
        Destroy(rectangle.gameObject);
    }
}

_rectangles.Clear();
}
```

Key Points

In this chapter, we unlocked new AI possibilities using Microsoft's Azure Cognitive Services APIs. We created an Azure Computer Vision client by providing the service key and endpoint we created previously. Then, we fed the service with Kinect's color frame data. The service contacted the Azure cloud and analyzed the image before returning an array of detected objects. The detected objects expose a set of properties, including their type and bounding rectangle. Using the bounding rectangle, we calculated each object's center and drew a 2D visual box around it. With the help of the Coordinate Mapper, we estimated the position of each object in the 3D world space. This way, we enhanced the AI results with depth measurements. By now, I hope you have a good foundation to explore the rest of Cognitive Service APIs, such as voice recognition, image classification, and optical character recognition.

Index

A

Angle() method, 206

Artificial intelligence (AI), 32, 39, 219, 232

Augmented Reality

    Azure Kinect color frame, 171

    body index map

        array, 176

        color frame acquisition, 176

        color to depth, 178–180, 182–185

        definition, 174

        structure, 175

        visualization, 178

    body pixels, 173

    definition, 169

    depth frame, 172

    depth-to-color alignment, 172

    physical /digital world, 170

    segmentation process, 170

    Unity 3D, 185, 187–189

    XBOX, 169

Azure, 220, 224, 232

Azure cognitive services, 232

    computer vision, 237, 242, 243

    importing, Unity3D

        binaries, 240

        project structure, 240

        subfolders, 239

    Microsoft, 221

    NuGet packages, 238, 239

    offline approach, 221, 222

    online approach, 222, 223

    REST, 237

    steps, 221

    Unity scene, 241, 242

    web-related methods, 237

Azure data centers, 220

Azure Kinect, 18

    SDK, 110, 180

    SDK's calibration methods, 166

Azure Kinect binaries, 18

    C# managed, 45, 46

    folders, 44, 45

    machine learning models, 48–50

    native C++, 47, 48

Azure Kinect Body Tracking SDK

    AMD and Intel, 33

    computers, 33

    CUDA toolkit, 33

    Microsoft, 32

    simple camera transformations, 32

    skeletal joints, 32

    system requirements, 33

    viewer, 34, 35

Azure Kinect depth sensor, 85

Azure Kinect Viewer

    acceleration, 28

    accelerometer and gyroscope

        readings, 29

    colorized 3D point cloud viewer, 30, 31

    device acceleration and rotation, 24

    infrared (IR) image, 26

    microphones, 29, 30

    Program Files, 23

    RGB color frame, 27, 28

V. Pterneas, *Mastering the Microsoft Kinect*, https://doi.org/10.1007/978-1-4842-8070-6

Printed in the United States
by Baker & Taylor Publisher Services